RECOVERING REDEMPTION

HOW CHRIST CHANGES EVERYTHING

MATT CHANDLER

LifeWay Press®
Nashville, Tennessee

Published by LifeWay Press®
© 2014 The Village Church

ISBN 9781430031970
Item 005644108

Dewey decimal classification: 234.3
Subject headings: SANCTIFICATION \ SALVATION \ SPIRITUAL LIFE

To order additional copies of this resource, write to LifeWay Church Resources Customer Service; One LifeWay Plaza; Nashville, TN 37234-0113; fax 615.251.5933; phone toll free 800.458.2772; order online at *www.lifeway.com;* email *orderentry@lifeway.com;* or visit the LifeWay Christian Store serving you.

Printed in the United States of America

Adult Ministry Publishing
LifeWay Church Resources
One LifeWay Plaza
Nashville, TN 37234-0152

CONTENTS

5   INTRODUCTION

6   SESSION 1   THE REALITY: EVERYTHING IS BROKEN

26   SESSION 2   THE REMEDY: OUR HOPE IN THE GOSPEL

44   SESSION 3   THE RESPONSE: FAITH & REPENTANCE

62   SESSION 4   THE RESULT: JUSTIFICATION & ADOPTION

78   SESSION 5   GROWING IN HOLINESS: SANCTIFICATION

94   SESSION 6   KNOWING OUR BROKENNESS: FREE FROM SHAME

110 SESSION 7   TRUSTING GOD'S GOODNESS: FREE FROM FEAR

126 SESSION 8   CONTINUING HEALTHY CYCLES: THE NEW SELF

140 SESSION 9   EXPERIENCING GRACE: LOVE & CONFESSION

158 SESSION 10   MAKING PEACE: CONFRONTING SIN

174 SESSION 11   PURSUING JOY: THE ABUNDANT LIFE

190 SESSION 12   SHARING HOPE: LIGHT OF THE WORLD

THE AUTHOR

MATT CHANDLER serves as the lead pastor of teaching at The Village Church in the Dallas/Fort Worth metroplex. He came to The Village in December 2002 and describes his tenure as a replanting effort to change the theological and philosophical culture of the congregation. The church has witnessed a tremendous response, growing from 160 people to more than 11,000, including campuses in Flower Mound, Dallas, Denton, and Fort Worth.

Alongside his current role as lead pastor, Matt is involved in church-planting efforts both locally and internationally through The Village, as well as in various strategic partnerships. Prior to accepting the pastorate at The Village, Matt had a vibrant itinerant ministry for more than 10 years that gave him the opportunity to speak to thousands of people in America and abroad about the glory of God and the beauty of Jesus.

Matt is also the author of *The Explicit Gospel Bible Study* (LifeWay, 2012) and a coauthor of *Creature of the Word* (LifeWay, 2012).

Other than knowing Jesus, Matt's greatest joy is being married to Lauren and being the dad to their three children, Audrey, Reid, and Norah.

INTRODUCTION

I don't know if you've noticed—I'm guessing you have—but the world is a mess. Things are broken. People are broken. And we run down different paths looking for answers. This is true for people both inside and outside the church. But the glorious reality of the gospel is this: Christ changes everything.

I don't just mean that He changed history or that He changes our eternal destiny. I don't even just mean that He will ultimately make everything right again in the future. Christ changes every part of your life and mine. Everything. Every day.

That's what *Recovering Redemption* is all about—walking through the questions we should all be asking and learning how the answers transform not only our minds but also our hearts and our day-to-day lives. No more settling for less than life abundant. No more treating symptoms instead of seeking health. It's time to grow up into spiritual maturity, living each day in the hope and freedom of Christ.

How to Get the Most from This Study

1. Attend each group experience.
• Watch the video teaching.
• Complete the viewer guide.
• Participate in the group discussions.

2. Complete the content in this Bible study book.
• Read the introduction for each session.
• Prayerfully interact with all learning activities.
• Be honest with God, yourself, and others about your experiences.
• Apply the principles.

3. Read Matt Chandler and Michael Snetzer's book *Recovering Redemption*.
• Optional chapters are noted in each session for taking you deeper into specific principles, unpacking the biblical truths and practical implications.

4. Commit to the experience.
• *Recovering Redemption* has 12 sessions with three components of personal study for each. Most groups will do this study over the course of 12 weeks, but if your group follows a different schedule, that's OK.
• Don't rush. Allow time for the Spirit of God to work in you through His Word.

THE REALITY: EVERYTHING IS BROKEN

SHARE WHAT GOD IS DOING. #RECOVERINGREDEMPTION

WELCOME TO YOUR FIRST SESSION OF RECOVERING REDEMPTION.
BEGIN DISCUSSION WITH THE ACTIVITY BELOW.

Take a minute for everyone to introduce themselves with a quick answer to one of the following questions:

What's the best news you've ever received, and what made it so good?

When have you made a mess trying to do something on your own before finally accepting help?

There's good news, and there's bad news. Always start with the bad news, right?

To fully appreciate the good news of the gospel—the joy and freedom it brings— we must first realize that we're living in the midst of bad news. We're swimming in it. Drowning. And until our eyes are opened to that fact, we don't realize our desperate need for salvation. When we feel the gravity of bad news, the good news is all the more glorious.

Here's the bad news: the world is busted up. The world you and I are living in is not the world as God created it.

What bad news or evidence of brokenness have you seen this week?

TO PREPARE FOR THE VIDEO, READ ALOUD ECCLESIASTES 1:14-15:

I have seen everything that is done under the sun, and behold, all is vanity and a striving after wind.
What is crooked cannot be made straight,
and what is lacking cannot be counted.

WATCH

COMPLETE THE VIEWER GUIDE BELOW AS YOU WATCH SESSION 1.

Gospel means _____ _____.

The world you and I are living in is not the world as God _____ it.

In Genesis 1–2 the triune God of the universe—God the Father, God the Son, God the Holy Spirit—in perfect contentment in the Godhead overflowed in their love and affection for one another onto the canvas of creation and _____ all that was.

God the Father is the _____ of creation.

God the Son is the active _____ of creation.

The Holy Spirit is the personal _____ of God that brings life to where there is no life.

At that moment outright _____ is declared against the King of glory, and the cosmos fractures.

_____ chaos was introduced when sin entered the world.

All we were meant to cultivate will now _____ against us.

We groan in eager longing, along with creation, for things to be _____.

FOUR PLACES WE RUN TO FIX THINGS

1. _____
You will never be good enough for _____.

2. _____
The fracture in the foundation of every relationship is "You will satisfy me and _____ me."

We find the fullness of life in _____, not in others.

3. The _____
Common grace is God's good gifts to _____.

When we run to the world outside the _____ of what God created things to be enjoyed in, we hamstring and hurt ourselves.

4. _____
Religion says, "I'm going to tilt the scales in my favor by being a _____ _____."

Video sessions available for purchase
at *www.lifeway.com/recoveringredemption*

DISCUSS THE VIDEO SEGMENT, USING THE QUESTIONS BELOW.

Although Genesis 1–3 may be familiar, what did you notice for the first time in this message?

Matt described Genesis 3:8 as the most heartbreaking verse in all Scripture. Why is it so tragic?

In what ways do you experience the ongoing brokenness of creation in everyday life? How do you see it at work? In your relationships? With your health?

Matt identified four empty wells we run to in our efforts to fill the cracks in our lives:

1. *Ourselves.* We strive to create a better version of ourselves to solve our discontent.

2. *Others.* We run to other people (spouses, children, friends) to complete us.

3. *The world.* We look to pleasures the world can provide (common graces), such as food or sex, to satisfy our souls.

4. *Religion.* We try to appease God or earn His favor through religious practices.

Which of these wells do you run to most often?

How have you experienced the emptiness of these wells?

As you go through the next week before our next group experience, try to notice when you're running down one of these crooked paths to dry wells that can never satisfy. Make a mental note or, better yet, write it down. What brought it on? How did you find yourself responding? What were you feeling at the time?

READ SESSION 1 AND COMPLETE THE PERSONAL STUDY BEFORE THE NEXT GROUP EXPERIENCE.

CONSIDER GOING DEEPER INTO THIS CONTENT BY READING CHAPTERS 1–2 IN MATT CHANDLER AND MICHAEL SNETZER'S BOOK RECOVERING REDEMPTION (B&H, 2014).

THE REALITY: EVERYTHING IS BROKEN

The world is busted up. Something's not right. We see that fact all around us. We see it within us.

For many, brokenness works itself out as depression, anxiety, fear, or addiction. Others stay busy achieving, indulging, chasing dreams, climbing ladders, or running away. Whether paralyzed or mobilized by it, we all either numb the feeling or grow numb ourselves.

When we feel that gnawing in our guts, that desire for something more— though we're not even sure what that "more" is—something in our souls remembers Genesis 1–2. There's a gaping hole within us that needs to be filled. We're cracked. Everything is broken. And so we groan with all creation in eager longing for restoration.

Our desire to fix this brokenness is the empirical data that we know things have gone wrong and need to be made right.

But we can't fix it, and believe it or not, recognizing that is good news!

1.1

GOD'S CREATION—IT WAS GOOD

And it was . . . good.

What an understatement!

The act of creation itself reads in the original language of the Old Testament with a pulsating cadence, almost like a musical rhythm: God created, it was good, God created, it was good, and everything He created was very good. Perfect harmony, characteristic of the triune Author of life, was written into every nuance of His work. A beauty and balance filled creation. The Hebrew language has a word for this sense of completeness, well-being, and soundness: *shalom*.

Peace.

His world was at perfect peace.

READ GENESIS 1:1–2:3.

Try to picture perfect peace. What does it look like? Sound like? Feel like?

What does this passage tell you about the order of creation—its purpose, goodness, and completeness?

What does this passage reveal to you about God? Think in terms of His nature and character.

What does it reveal to you about humankind and God's intent for us?

In the beginning this planet was once fresh and new. The same planet where you peel open the wrapper on a drive-through dinner while stuck in traffic. The one where you wake up stiff from working out or moaning yourself out of bed with whatever's knotted up overnight. The one where thoughts in your mind sail to dark places while you're standing in the checkout line. The one with terminal diagnoses, addictions, violence, natural disasters …

"Surely it doesn't have to be this way. This can't be right," you say. But there was a time when people never contemplated such things. Nothing in their world was dead or dying. Nothing was ominous or unsafe. Nothing was leaking, running late, unaffordable, or overwhelming. The weather was perfect, work was perfect, marriage was perfect, everything was perfect. Humans lived within the perfect freedom and fellowship existing between God, other people, and all creation.

That's how it was. That's how He created it.

READ GENESIS 2:8-9,15-25.

In what specific ways did God provide for Adam and Eve?

How is the Creator providing what you need in life? Think in terms of basic needs such as food and shelter as well as needs in your work and relationships.

The triune God of the universe—Father, Son, and Spirit—existing forever in perfect contentment with one another, overflowed with love and affection onto the canvas of creation.

God didn't need to do it. He didn't need you or anything else. That would imply He was somehow incomplete. God wasn't bored or lonely, needing somebody new to talk to, hang out with, or even to love. He wasn't dependent on an ego boost from subordinate creatures. On the contrary, the magnificent Three-in-One, lacking nothing, was delighted to express Himself with the powerful words that brought all things into existence.

How does a picture of God somehow needing to create mankind distort our view of God? Of ourselves? Of the world?

What was your earliest understanding of God? How has your view of God changed over time?

How does an accurate perspective of the triune God change the way you relate to Him? Pray? Worship?

God never needed people. People always needed God but not because they were originally sinful. They needed Him simply because they were human. He created us from the very beginning to live in a loving, dependent relationship with Him. That's His design.

God formed man from the dust of the ground, breathed life into his nostrils, hand-crafted woman from flesh and bone beside man, and He saw that it was good. Sin wasn't there. The Word of God begins where our understanding of the gospel needs to begin: with the peace, wholeness, and glory of creation. In the beginning God created, and it was good.

How does the context of Genesis 1–2 change your understanding of the good news of the gospel? Your understanding of life?

God planted a garden and created Adam and Eve to live and work together in it. Think about the environments where God has placed you to live out His design.

What relationships has He provided? And what implications does God's original design have for your relationships today?

Often work today is discussed as a necessary evil—something to pay the bills so that we can enjoy life on the weekends or when we retire. But in Genesis work is part of the perfect created order—before the curse of sin. Adam and Eve were first described as helpmates.

> How does viewing work as part of God's good design affect your attitude and lifestyle?

Genesis 2 ends with a beautiful description of life in harmony. All creation has been building, a crescendo of perfection, until these final words before the fall linger in time: "The man and his wife were both naked and were not ashamed" (Gen. 1:25). Nothing to hide. No reason to feel judgment or comparison. Complete. Content. Free. By God's design.

> How transparent are you with God? Rate your relationship below.

HIDING   FREE

> How transparent are you with people? Rate your relationships below.

HIDING   FREE

> Why did you rate your relationship with God and others as you did?

We'll look more at recovering the complete transparency and freedom we've lost. Today know that life isn't what it once was, but there's hope.

BEGIN YOUR PRAYER TIME BY PRAISING GOD AS CREATOR. ASK GOD TO HELP YOU TAKE SPECIFIC STEPS TO BECOME MORE TRANSPARENT AND TRUTHFUL WITH HIM AND WITH OTHER PEOPLE YOU CAN TRUST.

I.2

THE FALL—OUR BROKENNESS

God gave Adam and Eve just one rule. It wasn't complex.

They'd been placed within the pristine wonders of Eden, invited by God's design into a life of no shame, no hiding, no fear, no secrets, no need for sneaking around, nothing at all to worry about. They'd been given pleasant work to do. They'd been given each other, without so much as a stitch of clothes between them. And they'd been given an abundance of options for food, with only one distinct exclusion—the one tree whose fruit, if they ate of it, could be counted on to kill them.

That wasn't heavy-handed. That was a pretty sweet deal.

How can boundaries be loving and lead to freedom?

How do we see obedience and joy being woven into the canvas of a perfect creation?

READ GENESIS 3:1-6.

What is Satan's purpose in temptation? How does questioning God's goodness play into temptation? Questioning God's authority? Questioning what we deserve?

What followed mankind's act of defiance was literally world-changing. Everything screeched violently out of sync from the rhythm and harmony of God's original design. Rebellion had been declared against the King of glory. Everything was broken. Everything is still broken.

READ GENESIS 3:7-13.

The immediate effects of sin are shame and blame.

> How do people hide from God (and each other) because of shame?

> Of what are you ashamed? What specific areas in your life are you covering up and wanting to hide from God and/or others?

Shame isn't something of which we have to be convinced. We feel it. We know it's there, and we hate it.

Blame is harder to admit because, by definition, it's a form of denial. It's our go-to defense mechanism. We try to lift the soul-crushing burden of shame off ourselves by passing blame. Notice that in Genesis 3 nobody owned up to what they did. "It was that woman you gave me." "It was that serpent." Nobody's ever responsible. This creates havoc. Relationships are blown up.

> Sin isn't accidental. You choose it. Even if considered for a split-second, there's always an excuse made to justify sin. Think of sin in your life. Whom or what do you usually blame?

> Identify a specific person and situation that you've affected by shifting blame. Has blame ever solved a sin problem? How has blame affected your relationships?

Like a bomb, sin rips through our world, rattling the balance of creation and fracturing humanity at our core. Sin and brokenness are inseparable. The Bible boils down the damage report to two universal categories of consequence: futility and pain.

FUTILITY. Paul said creation was "subjected to futility" (Rom. 8:20). That word conveys the idea of being hard-pressed, shoved down, confined, restricted. What had once been peaceful and prosperous has now been turned into strain and struggle. Every effort faces resistance. Every drop of energy can be wrung out of us, and it seems we still don't have enough to get through the day, the week, or the month.

PAIN. More specifically, the Bible refers to the particular pain of childbirth (see Rom. 8:22). The intense pain of childbirth, both literal and figurative, is a direct result of what sin has brought into our world. Suffering saturates daily life.

We know from reading the aftermath of the fallout in Genesis 3 that the hits just keep on coming. Relational chaos. Work difficulties. And ultimately, death (see Jas. 1:15). It began with Adam and Eve and has been passed down to every generation since, a domino effect of fallen creatures.

What Adam and Eve began, we have continued—and we can't help continuing. We've joined them in rebellion (see Rom. 5:12). How have you experienced this to be true?

Why do you think it's so hard for people to be transparent and truthful about themselves? What keeps us from coming out of the trees and being vulnerable?

What hope exists in Genesis 3? How do you see God seeking fellowship with Adam and Eve, even after their rebellion? What does this reveal about God's love for you?

The Bible encourages us to confess our sins to God (see Lev. 5:5) and to one another (see Jas. 5:16). Proverbs 28:13 says:

> *Whoever conceals his transgressions will not prosper,*
> *but he who confesses and forsakes them will obtain mercy.*

Take a moment now to confess your sins to God. Then write down the name of a godly friend whom you trust and commit to being transparent with that person.

READ PSALM 51.

How would you characterize King David's attitude in this psalm? (If you aren't familiar with the sinfulness over which David is lamenting, you can read 2 Sam. 11–12.)

What glaring differences exist between the response of David (see Ps. 51) and that of Adam and Eve (see Gen. 3)?

What do you learn from David and his attitude toward the seriousness of sin?

PRAY THE WORDS OF DAVID IN PSALM 51. AS YOU DO, BEGIN BY HUMBLY ADMITTING YOUR REBELLIOUS ATTITUDES. DROP YOUR DEFENSES. SURRENDER THE BLAME. CONFESS YOUR SINS TO GOD. THANK JESUS FOR BLOTTING OUT YOUR INIQUITY ON THE CROSS AND, BY DOING SO, CREATING A NEW, PURE HEART INSIDE OF YOU.

1.3

EMPTY EFFORTS—FOUR QUICK FIXES

We're fixers.

None of us can escape the underlying sense of displeasure and disappointment in life. We may not feel it as acutely every day, but it's experienced often enough that each of us rears up with the urge to do something about it, to get out from under the weight, to pick up the pieces, and to fix it.

As we search for relief, we typically run down four primary paths for a quick fix. But they're all crooked, dead-end paths leading to empty wells.

What you'll see in the four crooked paths you're about to examine is that no matter how much progress you may feel like you're making, no matter what temporary relief you experience in distancing yourself from some pain or discomfort, none of the paths ultimately arrive at wholeness. There are no shortcuts. No alternative routes. None of these paths will ever lead to freedom. None of the wells from which you draw will ever fill you to satisfaction. The temporary quenching of your thirst is only a mirage, baiting you to travel further down the dead-end road. The wells dry up, and you hit rock bottom, trapped deep in the hole you've been digging.

We're fixers who can't truly fix anything.

So, it's time for a reality check. No hiding or passing the blame. Get gut-level honest about the four (wrong) places we all run to fix our brokenness.

1. OURSELVES

Hard to believe it, based on our sketchy track record, but we've thoroughly convinced ourselves that the cure for what's wrong with us is a better version of ourselves. Somewhere in our heads is a future person who's the embodiment of self-disciplined, self-defined perfection, that ideal self who'll turn our whole world right side up.

Here's a little diagnostic test: 10 years ago, what did you expect your life to be like at this point? Write as many specifics as possible (personal, professional, relational, recreational, educational).

Did you have a different picture of who you'd be by now? Do you wonder what happened to that person? If you haven't been able to become that new-and-improved you by now, after all this time, what makes you think you're going to become that person by tomorrow? Next year? Ever?

On a scale of 1 to 5 (5 = perfect), how happy are you with yourself? _____

On the same scale, how satisfied are you right now with each of the following areas of your life?

Your time management _____

Your work _____

Your free time _____

Your self-control _____

Your habits _____

Your appearance _____

Your health _____

Your dedication _____

Your ability level _____

Your talents _____

Your success _____

What do your scores tell you about yourself?

We can't redeem ourselves.

List specific ways you try to fix your own life, seeking a better self as the path to happiness and satisfaction.

READ JEREMIAH 17:5-9.

What does Jeremiah say is inevitable for all who rely on themselves? What's revealed about our hearts?

On the other hand, what's promised for the person who trusts the Lord?

Jeremiah asked a rhetorical question about the heart in verse 9: "Who can understand it?" How can God's response in verse 10 (that He knows our hearts and minds) give us hope in the midst of a bad situation?

2. OTHERS

Every relationship we enter will struggle and fail whenever we make the other person into a god who's supposed to make us complete.

Men make terrible gods. Women make terrible gods. Children make terrible gods. Friends, colleagues, teammates, parents, boyfriends/girlfriends—you name it. Whenever you expect people to fill the cracks that are gaping open in your heart, you're moving not in the direction of freedom and healing, not into fullness and satisfaction, but down a dark well of conflict and chaos.

The expectation that others can somehow become for us the answer to all our problems is to put an impossible weight on them that they were never intended or equipped to carry. It's going to make life miserable for everybody.

Everyone is jacked up. Everyone has issues. How crazy is it to expect other broken people to fix and rescue you or anyone else?

Others simply can't redeem us.

READ DEUTERONOMY 4:35-40.

Why does God repeat that we must have no other gods before Him? What does that say about our hearts? What does it say about God's desire for us and our relationship with Him?

READ PSALM 146:3-10.

What logical reasons does the psalmist give for why we shouldn't put our trust in other people, regardless of earthly status? And in contrast, how does the LORD prove His faithfulness?

READ ACTS 4:12.

Who are you tempted to prop up as a god to fix you and give your life meaning and value? Apply the phrase "no other name" to your own circumstances. Jot down some names—spouse, boyfriend/girlfriend, parent, child(ren), friends, pastor—specific people you may rely on for self-worth: There's no other name, not _____ or _____ or _____, by which I can be saved.

3. THE WORLD

Another path we recklessly wander down, thinking the solution to all our problems is waiting just over the next hill, is the one filled with the world's pleasures.

One of the biggest lies about this empty well is that the road is paved only with socially taboo evils. But any of the inherently pleasurable things in this world, given freely as good gifts from a loving Father, can be abused and misused. Settling for anything as sufficient for our happiness, rather than enjoying the Giver of the gift, is idolatry.

When we buy new stuff—maybe with money we don't even have—because it makes us feel we've accomplished something …

When we take that bite—maybe one more bite—believing it will bring satisfaction to an otherwise mundane or stressful experience …

When we're dying for sex—maybe with someone new this time—hoping it will calm jittery insecurities …

We're elevating created things above their Creator.

But the world doesn't have what's needed to redeem us.

READ DEUTERONOMY 6:10-12.

What did God promise the Israelites entering the promised land? What was God's part in supplying for them? What was their part?

What are some ways you've "forgotten" the Lord after He brought you out of some bondage and blessed you with good things?

READ MATTHEW 6:19-21,24,33.

What do these verses reveal to you about money, possessions, and God? What warnings are there for your heart? What promise does God give you?

List specific things in this world that you're tempted to overvalue. What do you chase while contentment seems just out of reach?

4. RELIGION

This one can be the most deceptive path. It knows all the right things to say and do at all the right times. It can be cheered on and admired by well-meaning individuals, small groups, or even churches. It could even have you leading this small group. Religion may be the most dangerous well to draw from, because it can appear to be the life God desires for us. The problem is under the surface. The issue is motivation.

If we're honest, the shocking truth is that religion is just a better version of you (see number 1) with a choir robe on and shouting, "Amen!" You are seeking to create self-worth and acceptance by proving your devotion. You're trying to tip the scales in your favor by doing one more good thing. But your Heavenly Father isn't looking to be impressed by your report card. Your trophies will never earn His approval and affection. He already loves you. Unconditionally.

> In your experience how long do your best efforts at devotion quench your thirst for the loving approval of a Heavenly Father?

Religion doesn't work. You can never be redeemed by religion.

READ ISAIAH 64:6-8.

> How does Isaiah describe the value of religious acts?

> What does the potter-and-clay illustration reveal about your relationship with God? What's your role? How can you be fixed?

READ ISAIAH 1:11-20.

> How does God feel about trying to tip cosmic scales in your favor without a genuine relationship? What good does religious activity do?

List specific ways you busily draw from the empty well of religious activity.

Don't worry; there's good news coming. But the truth is that you can't fix yourself. That has to sink in. Feel the gravity of your need.

The answer to your problem isn't at the bottom of any of the four wells we all run to. They hold no lasting satisfaction. Be aware this week of the ways you run down crooked paths to empty wells. Prayerfully remind yourself that you're designed to be completely dependent on your Creator and then trust your loving Father.

READ THE CONCLUDING SCRIPTURE TO GUIDE YOUR PRAYER:

> *My people have committed two evils:*
> *they have forsaken me,*
> > *the fountain of living waters,*
> *and hewed out cisterns for themselves,*
> > *broken cisterns that can hold no water.*
>
> **JEREMIAH 2:13**

AS YOU PRAY, RECOGNIZE THAT ALL YOUR ATTEMPTS AT REDEMPTION AMOUNT TO FORSAKING GOD AND POURING YOUR BEST HOPES INTO "BROKEN CISTERNS THAT CAN HOLD NO WATER." THIS IS THE FIRST STEP DOWN THE ONLY PATH LEADING TO PEACE AND FREEDOM.

THE REMEDY: OUR HOPE IN THE GOSPEL

SHARE WHAT GOD IS DOING. #RECOVERINGREDEMPTION

BEGIN DISCUSSION WITH THE ACTIVITY BELOW.

At the end of our previous group experience, we were encouraged to watch out for temptations to go to one of four empty wells—*ourselves*, *others*, *the world*, or *religion*. These are all futile attempts at filling the cracks in our lives.

Which well did you find yourself drawing from throughout the week?

What makes the path to that well an easy one for you to wander down looking for a remedy?

What else struck you in your personal study of creation and the fall?

Today is good news! In this session we'll answer the big question raised by the bad news of our reality: is there any hope? There is a remedy.

TO PREPARE FOR THE VIDEO, READ ALOUD PSALM 40:11-17:

> *As for you, O LORD, you will not restrain your mercy from me;*
> *your steadfast love and your faithfulness will ever preserve me!*
> *For evils have encompassed me beyond number;*
> *my iniquities have overtaken me, and I cannot see;*
> *they are more than the hairs of my head; my heart fails me.*
> *Be pleased, O LORD, to deliver me!*
> *O LORD, make haste to help me! ...*
> *May all who seek you rejoice and be glad in you;*
> *may those who love your salvation say continually, "Great is the LORD!"*
> *As for me, I am poor and needy, but the Lord takes thought for me.*
> *You are my help and my deliverer; do not delay, O my God!*

WATCH

COMPLETE THE VIEWER GUIDE BELOW AS YOU WATCH SESSION 2.

For news to be good, it has to invade _____ _____.

WAYS PEOPLE GO WHEN THEY REALIZE THEY'RE UNCLEAN

1. _____

You don't do sinful acts to make yourself a _____. You are a sinner, so you do sinful _____.

Behavioral modification isn't going to work, because whatever reigns and rules in your _____ will overflow out of your heart into your actions and attitudes.

2. _____

No one can make you think _____ thoughts.

The real issue isn't our marriage, our addiction, our struggle, our loneliness, our depression, our lust but our _____.

God _____ the weak. He oftentimes saves and uses the weak to shame the _____.

By the death of Jesus Christ, we have been _____. We have been made right.

We are given new _____ by the God of the universe. We are given new _____ in that new heart.

While you were enemies, Christ _____ for you.

When you were at your weakest, at the appointed time God _____ you.

I'm habitually laying my life before the Lord and asking for His help to _____ the gospel all the more, to _____ Him, and to _____ _____ the implications of the gospel in my life.

We were rescued and saved by _____ alone through _____ alone. God gets the _____ alone.

I'm completely set free from the slavery of _____.

We don't do things to get God to love us. We do those things because He does love us, and we are in pursuit of growing in greater _____ with the Savior of our souls.

Video sessions available for purchase
at *www.lifeway.com/recoveringredemption*

DISCUSS THE VIDEO SEGMENT, USING THE QUESTIONS BELOW.

What questions, new insights, or takeaways do you have from the video?

How do the bad news from session 1 and the good news of session 2 fit together as corrective lenses to rightly view our lives?

Jesus revealed that what makes us unclean is already inside us (see Mark 7). What fresh perspective has seeing that "the heart of the problem is the problem of the heart" provided?

In Romans 5:6 Paul assures us that while we were weak, powerless, and utterly helpless on our own, Christ died for us—at just the right time.

So what was the right time for you? Describe when God rescued you and the ways you were weak and powerless at that time.

Think again about the four empty wells we run to for salvation: *ourselves*, *others*, *the world*, and *religion*. How does the gospel dethrone each of these false gods?

Matt talked about his marriage to illustrate the distinction between religion—that is, trying to earn God's favor by being a good person—and discipline, such as getting up early to spend time with God in prayer, study His Word, and memorize Scripture.

What has been your past motivation for spiritual discipline? How does the illustration of a healthy relationship encourage you to look at personal motivation and discipline in knowing God?

What will you do this week to know God and pursue greater intimacy with Him?

READ SESSION 2 AND COMPLETE THE PERSONAL STUDY BEFORE THE NEXT GROUP EXPERIENCE.

CONSIDER GOING DEEPER INTO THIS CONTENT BY READING CHAPTER 3 IN MATT CHANDLER AND MICHAEL SNETZER'S BOOK RECOVERING REDEMPTION (B&H, 2014).

THE REMEDY: OUR HOPE IN THE GOSPEL

We're all broken from the fall. We all inherit a deep lack of satisfaction. We feel unclean. But we can never fix it or clean it up. At best, we only smear the mess.

But this inability and lack of satisfaction can be a gift from God.

How?

It drives us to our knees, desperate for the redemption found only in the gospel.

The bad news of the previous session is invaded and conquered by the good news of Jesus Christ's victory and the freedom He brings to everyone in His kingdom. Our Heavenly Father doesn't leave His children unclean and in their sinful mess. By His strength, He leads them out of it. So it's OK to not be OK—it's just not OK to stay there.

God, by His resurrected Son, in the power of the Holy Spirit, transforms your life for His magnificent purposes. He makes you clean. He rescues you. He gets the glory.

This is the gospel.

2.1

THE ROOT OF THE ISSUE—WE'RE UNCLEAN

One day it happens. We wake up to the fact that we're not clean. And there's nothing we can do to clean ourselves up.

After all efforts at filling the cracks in our lives have failed, we find ourselves in an overwhelming mess. Whatever magic cure we hoped to find at the bottom of those wells didn't deliver on its promise. But our natural response is still fixated on cleaning up the surface of our lives. Ignoring the root of sin manifests itself in two major ways that were introduced last week: religion and blame.

Let's start by remembering what is meant by *religion*.

Religion is always outside-in. It's the belief that an act of devotion will make you clean, countering the belief that an act of deviance made you unclean. It's a spiritual bartering system: "I'll do something for You, God, and You do something for me." But come on. Surely you see how backward that is.

READ MARK 7:1-13.

What root issue was Jesus addressing?

The Scripture describes religious people obsessing over (and judging others by) strict traditions and moral loopholes rather than focusing on God's Word and the heart of His people. In what ways have you ever wrongly measured yourself by human standards? Judged others?

How can religious rules and traditions become a substitute for a sincere relationship with God?

How can acts of worship, service, and moral standards be part of a healthy spiritual life?

The people Jesus was teaching in this passage had dietary and cleanliness laws. There were certain foods they couldn't eat and certain ways they had to wash hands, dishes, and even furniture. They literally believed that something outside them could somehow make their souls dirty. Impurity before God was contagious; it could spread like any other contamination. Touching, eating, or even walking by something unclean would make a person unholy. But Jesus made it clear: "No, no, no. That's not how it works. What's unclean is already inside you."

READ MARK 7:14-23.

Summarize what Jesus teaches about where sin does and doesn't begin.

What's the effect of viewing the root of sin as external? As internal?

We often get things backward in our spiritual lives. Let's be clear: that activity you participate in that you feel ashamed of—that's not what's made you unclean. You're unclean, so you did that activity. You don't do sinful acts to make yourself a sinner. You're a sinner, so you do sinful acts.

What specific sins do you tend to fixate on in other people's lives, judging them as untouchable? How does what you wrote above—about the root of sin—affect your view of other people? Of yourself?

What happens when your focus is solely on changing wrong behavior— the symptomatic fruit of sin?

REREAD VERSES 21-22.

Identify some things in your life that make you feel unclean. Specifically, how will you reorient your perspective to view your sin as Jesus does?

As you saw in the last session, religion gets deceptively close to genuine relationship. But it's external and surface. And just as it didn't work for the religious leaders of Jesus' day, it's not going to fix you today. It never can, because whatever reigns from the throne of your heart will work itself out through your actions and attitudes. Externally motivated religion still has you in the driver's seat. You may be letting religious guidelines plot your moral course, but if you're still white-knuckling the steering wheel, it's still your own effort. Religion waves the banner of God's name with one hand and tries to do the very thing He saved us from with the other hand.

If the heart of the problem really is the problem of the heart, how effective are attempts at moral tinkering and behavior modification?

Based on your personal struggles, what in your life are you putting in God's place?

Jesus didn't provide a direct solution to the problem of the heart in this passage. What might be the reason He didn't give an answer?

It hurts. It gets uncomfortable. The closer we get to the Light, the more dirt we're going to see. Sometimes we just honestly don't want to hear the truth about our sin.

So the other way we ignore the root of our problem is blame.

If nothing outside you can make you unclean, that includes other people. It's simple logic. No one else can even make you think evil thoughts. No one. What's inside you is all yours. You might be thinking that's not true: *You don't know what happened.* Or: *You don't know this person. See, if you knew so-and-so, you wouldn't be saying that. Because they make me … that makes me …*

No.

Your choices are your choices. Your thoughts are your thoughts. Period.

People can betray you. People can hurt you. And they will. They've already done some damage. You're wrecked from past collisions. Yet no one controls what you think but you. By the power of God's Spirit, you can arrest those runaway thoughts. You can say, "No, that's not true; that's not right. I'm not going there or dwelling on that." You decide what you fixate on. You decide the fantasies in your mind. You decide whether you're going to pray for someone and forgive them. You choose whether you'll park in bitterness, wishing for revenge. You decide.

What recurring thought(s) seems unshakable and out of your control?

Whom or what do you tend to blame for those thoughts?

How are your actions related to your thoughts?

Again, can people around you do wicked things? Absolutely. And can other people inflict serious wounds? For sure. And to some degree we'll experience this collateral damage of a broken world filled with broken people. But that's external—it's outside you. Ultimately, everyone has to answer to God. Including you. Nobody's excusing anybody's behavior or making light of how it hurt you. Later in the series we'll focus specifically on relationships. For now, knowing you can't change the past and can't control others, the starting point is with you and how you'll move forward in freedom.

The heart of your problem is the problem of your heart.

You're fractured at your core.

Nothing outside you makes you unclean. Nobody outside you is responsible for your mind. Deep down it's your heart that's the issue. That's the root of it all. No amount of moral tinkering, religious activity, or behavior modification will clean you up inside. Nobody else can be blamed. Not for your part. You have to own it. And you can't fix it. That's heavy. But it turns you around and puts you on a path to freedom.

FINALLY, READ JOHN 10:10.

> How do Jesus' words in John 10:10 show us that the desire for more in life can be a good gift from God? What remedy does Jesus offer?

IN PRAYER SURRENDER YOUR OWN WAYS OF THINKING AND DEALING WITH SIN. ASK GOD TO LEAD YOU TO UNDERSTAND THE WAYS OF YOUR HEART AND TO SET YOUR MIND ON HIM.

2.2

THE REMEDY FOR SIN

People ask, "So are you saying we're all just damned? There's nothing we can do to fix this problem we're in? That's it? From the moment we're born?" Yeah, that's pretty much what we're saying.

"So we can't really change? We're not capable of living the right way? We can't see what's wrong for ourselves and do what it takes to correct it?" Nope. That's the deal.

Unless . . .

. . . unless God steps into the shattered glass of your broken marriage—hopelessly beyond repair—and shows you what the gospel provides in a fully redeemed relationship.

. . . unless God plunges into the depths of your depression—never scolding your inability to shake loose from the emotional snare—and untangles you with relentless mercy.

. . . unless God shines the light of Christ into your mess through a loyal friend—when you saw yourself as dirty, despised, and disrespected—and welcomes you without condition as a child of the King.

. . . unless God reaches out to save you from yourself—even when everything in this world keeps falling apart—and gives you an eternal inheritance.

The beauty of Christ's gospel is the great "unless" of life.

Complete this sentence: my life is without hope unless . . .

READ ROMANS 5:1-11.

The word *therefore* refers back to Romans 3:21–28, where the apostle Paul declared our salvation to be through faith in Christ alone rather than through any religious deeds. Every verse in between (Rom. 3:29–4:25) has illustrated the fact that no great works could ever justify someone before God, not even respected men like Abraham. Here Paul wrote about the blessings of that salvation through faith.

What blessings (past, present, and future) do you see in the text?

At one time we were each God's enemies (see v. 10), but now we have peace with Him. Write a prayer thanking God for the peace He initiated and established with you. Be specific about why you're thankful.

How would you describe the hope and joy found in Christ, distinguishing them from happiness found elsewhere?

Write three ways you can have joy, being grateful for what God has already and ultimately done, even when you're suffering.

At just the right time God snatched you up. He used someone to bring you the hope of the gospel. Maybe that person incessantly annoyed you with it until you gave in. Maybe it was a subtler characteristic that intrigued you—some deeper longing that drew you to the hope in that person's life. The gospel became more than words on a page; it became your breath and your source of new life. When you were an enemy of God, dead in your rebellion, He snatched you up and rescued you. He brought you out of darkness and into the kingdom of light.

Christ intervened at the perfect point in history (see Gal. 4:4) and in your life as an individual. God's plan is flawless. He has redeemed each person "at the right time."

> What does this tell you about God's sovereignty—the fact that He's in control?

> Did you share your testimony in the group about your "at the right time" experience with God? If not, why not? If so, how comfortable were you, and what did you learn by sharing it?

> What stood out to you most about other group members' testimonies? What did you learn about God's love and power through their stories?

> What doubts have you wrestled with regarding your spiritual growth and salvation? Identify your darkest point, writing it down if you can.

God loved you even at your darkest. Scripture promises that while we were still His enemies, Christ loved us and died for us. If He loved you even when you were running away and fighting against Him, why wouldn't He love you now while you stumble along in your growth toward maturity?

> Keeping that promise in mind, how will you respond to feelings of unworthiness and uncleanness?

"Christianity is a crutch," people say. "It's for the weak." They mean this condescendingly, but it's true. Let's just admit that right here and now.

Christianity is a crutch because our legs are broken and we need something stronger than ourselves to lean on. We're all weak; none of us have the strength and ability to pull ourselves upright from our brokenness. Christians recognize this. It's nothing to be ashamed of. In fact, until we embrace it, we can never experience the freedom and healing power of the gospel.

READ 2 CORINTHIANS 12:7B-10.

For what reasons did Paul boast, and why was he content with his weakness (some versions translate "content" as "delight in")?

In your own words, how would you explain this Christian sense of being weak and boasting in Christ?

Where are you prone to pride? Write down two or three areas where you need to become weaker so that Christ's power can rest on you.

How have you experienced His power in your life?

(If you use social media, share what God has done for you and see what He is doing in other people's lives. #RecoveringRedemption)

AS YOU PRAY, THANK GOD FOR SAVING YOU AS YOU WERE—IN YOUR WEAKNESS, IN YOUR SIN, AT THE RIGHT TIME. THANK HIM FOR HIS CONTINUED LOVE AND ACCEPTANCE OF YOU, THOUGH YOU STILL DON'T EARN IT OR DESERVE IT. THANK HIM FOR HIS GRACE, WHICH IS SUFFICIENT FOR YOU EVEN IN THE MIDST OF THE WEAKNESSES, INSULTS, HARDSHIPS, PERSECUTIONS, AND CALAMITIES THAT MAY COME.

2.3

THE RESPONSE OF SALVATION

You've been made right. In your active rebellion against God, at the right time, Christ died for you.

When you see the root of sin and the remedy for sin, you have to respond. If you still struggle with being able to run hard after the Lord because you feel unworthy, Scripture reminds you that when you were at your worst, weak as you were and the enemy of God, at that moment God took the initiative, intervened, and rescued you.

And here's where it gets even more beautiful. He begins to straighten out those crooked paths you keep running down. Those dry wells that never satisfied are replaced with living water, overflowing from an eternal spring and flooding your life.

READ ROMANS 5:9-11.

> Salvation is more than a one-time experience; it's an ongoing blessing. Using the phrase below and Paul's pattern of piling God's blessings on top of blessings, fill in specific ways God has been gracious to you.
>
> If it weren't enough that God _____,
>
> even more, He continues to _____!
>
> And even more than that, He _____!

LOOK BACK AT ROMANS 5:5. ALSO SEE JOHN 16:7,12-14; GALATIANS 2:20; AND HEBREWS 7:24-25.

> How does Christ save us through His life, death, and resurrection?

For some reason we can hear stories of rescue and perseverance, we can hear the gospel truth proclaimed, and we still feel that our personal attempts at redemption stand a better chance of working out for us. This time, we tell ourselves, it'll work.

It's madness. And yet if we're really listening to the gospel, we begin to slow down our excuses and our reflexes long enough to acclimate to a whole new level of hope found in Christ. Then we may start to forget about those leaky buckets we lug to empty wells for a quick fix. That's when we start seeing some real change.

> When we respond to Christ in faith, these crooked paths start to straighten out. Brokenness and empty promises are replaced with hope and freedom. Read what the gospel has done to save you, and then write your personal response.

Yourself. You were saved by grace alone through faith alone. Therefore, God alone gets all the glory. And when you understand this one basic truth, you'll stop going to yourself and start going to the Lord—just laying out all your dirty laundry; shaking out all the stuff hidden deep in your pockets; bringing it all out into the open; and saying, "I can't do anything with the mess I've made. Only You can make me clean." This position creates humility and cuts the legs out from under a prideful swagger. There's no room for boasting. You didn't do anything. God saved you.

> How does the gospel give you hope, freeing you from *yourself*?

Others. A lot of us swing up or down almost solely on the basis of others' acceptance and affirmation. We need validation. When we get it, we're good. But if not, then we're nervous and self-conscious or moody and unhappy, even unable to function.

But your approval comes from God, not from your friends, coworkers, competitors, or critics—because at best, their opinions have a very limited shelf life. Those people are one step closer to death today, just like you are. The only approval that should matter to you is from the One you'll stand before in judgment someday. He's not only Judge, He's also Father. And He's already redeemed you. You've been bought with a price. What value can anyone give to you greater than what's already been paid by the Father—the precious blood of His Son?

> How does the gospel give you hope, freeing you from *others*?

The world. By means of the gospel, through which God has chosen to delight in us and has given us all things to enjoy—within the healthy, discerning boundaries of wisdom and common sense—every gift of common grace represents a fresh, new opportunity for us to celebrate His wonder, His mercy, and His glory. He's the One—not our ample income or our remarkably good looks—who's responsible for these blessings. He's the One who created in His world such a wide palette of flavors and textures, of aromas and pleasures. And so He's the One to be worshiped, thanked, and glorified every time we experience even the most basic of His material gifts.

When properly viewed within this gospel frame, neither your desire for these things nor your expected payoff of what they can do for you terminates on the gift itself. Rather, they roll up from pleasure into praise and gratitude for a Creator and Father who's the Giver of all good and perfect gifts. And you're totally satisfied. Only in Him.

How does the gospel give you hope, freeing you from *the world*?

Religion. There are no scales to be tipped in your favor. Thanks to the gospel, you don't need to prove anything to God. You aren't paying back any debt. You aren't earning any gold stars. You simply seek to enjoy even greater intimacy with Him, to get even closer to His heart, to open more and more of those inner closets where you've tried to restrict His access, thinking He wouldn't like what He sees, thinking He might reject you if He knew.

The reason you study His Word, attack your sin, generously share your resources, and serve the people around you isn't to persuade Him to love you. You do these things because He already loves you. You're so full from all He's pouring into you that you can't keep it from overflowing onto even seemingly ordinary tasks. You rejoice in it all.

How does the gospel give you hope, freeing you from *religion*?

The psalmist vividly summarized the bad news and the good news of our predicament:

> I waited patiently for the LORD;
> he inclined to me and heard my cry.
> He drew me up from the pit of destruction,
> out of the miry bog,
> and set my feet upon a rock,
> making my steps secure.
> He put a new song in my mouth,
> a song of praise to our God.
> Many will see and fear,
> and put their trust in the LORD.
> Blessed is the man who makes
> the LORD his trust,
> who does not turn to the proud,
> to those who go astray after a lie!
> You have multiplied, O LORD my God,
> your wondrous deeds and your thoughts toward us;
> none can compare with you!
> I will proclaim and tell of them,
> yet they are more than can be told.

PSALM 40:1–5

You can't pull yourself up by the bootstraps. You can't be fixed or validated by others, the world's experiences, or religious activity. Chasing those lies will lead you astray every time. Psalm 40 is wonderfully clear. No matter how desperately and sincerely you try, nothing could ever make you clean while living in a miry bog. Nothing could set you free. That empty well you ran to was a pit of destruction. Only the Lord could pull you out of the muck and mire.

You were stuck. He unstuck you. You were dirty. He made you clean. You were rescued by grace alone through faith alone. God alone gets the glory.

AS YOU ENTER YOUR PRAYER TIME, CONSIDER HOW YOUR BEST EFFORTS TO CLEAN YOURSELF UP HAVE ONLY SMEARED THE MESS. READ THE REST OF PSALM 40, PRAYING THE WORDS BACK TO GOD.

THE RESPONSE: FAITH & REPENTANCE

BEGIN DISCUSSION WITH THE ACTIVITY BELOW.

How did your time with God go this week? Did you try anything different in terms of your motivation or discipline?

What made the biggest impression on you during your personal study of session 2?

How did you respond to the gospel message as you considered the well you've been running to? What hope does the gospel provide? What empty promise does it replace?

What first comes to mind when you hear the word *repentance?* Is it positive, negative, or irrelevant?

We've seen that at our best, we just smear the mess. We can't clean ourselves up or fix our root problem. In this session we move from the work God has done to save us to what we do in response. A truly life-changing response to the gospel includes faith and repentance.

TO PREPARE FOR THE VIDEO, READ ALOUD PSALM 32:1-5:

Blessed is the one whose transgression is forgiven,
whose sin is covered.
Blessed is the man against whom the LORD counts no iniquity,
and in whose spirit there is no deceit.
For when I kept silent, my bones wasted away
through my groaning all day long.
For day and night your hand was heavy upon me;
my strength was dried up as by the heat of summer.
I acknowledged my sin to you,
and I did not cover my iniquity;
I said, "I will confess my transgressions to the LORD,"
and you forgave the iniquity of my sin.

COMPLETE THE VIEWER GUIDE BELOW AS YOU WATCH SESSION 3.

The fruit of faith is _____.

There is a type of sorrow that is godly, that leads to repentance and salvation without _____.

Worldly sorrow leads to _____.

WORLDLY GRIEF

1. Almost always _____
2. Purely emotional and not _____
3. Passive toward the _____ of grief
4. Full of _____ and avoids responsibilities and consequences

GODLY GRIEF

1. Has _____
The Word of God is _____. It's going to cut; it's going to reveal; it's going to show us where our rebellion is.

2. Leads to the gift of _____

3. Has to be _____

Godly sorrow is _____.

The most common place sorrow works itself out is in _____.

4. Has an element of _____
The shame we feel under the weight of God's holiness is not a type of shame that leads us into sin but rather a type of shame that leads us _____.

5. Produces a _____ for sin

6. Leads us to _____ and a life without regret

Video sessions available for purchase at *www.lifeway.com/recoveringredemption*

DISCUSS THE VIDEO SEGMENT, USING THE QUESTIONS BELOW.

What struck you in the teaching?

Matt talked about some of the ridiculous things people have said about what makes them a Christian (where they grew up, living in a Christian home, or going to church programs). What similar assumptions have you had about being a Christian?

Whom do you relate to most: the woman who anointed Jesus' feet (see Luke 7), the prodigal son (see Luke 15), or Zacchaeus (see Luke 19)?
  Why do you connect with their stories?
  What hope do they provide?
  How did they, in their own unique ways, show true repentance?

Matt discussed four worldly ways we show grief over sin: (1) horizontally, (2) emotionally, (3) passively, and (4) full of pride and blame. Did you sense him talking directly to you in any of those four ways of responding to sin? If so, which ones were most insightful or convicting?

Second Corinthians 7:10 says, "Godly grief produces a repentance that leads to salvation without regret, whereas worldly grief produces death." How do you recognize the difference in your own life between these two kinds of grief?

Matt said, "Oh, that we might be a people who embrace the confession of sins among one another for the good of our own souls and for the glory of God." How well are we doing as a group at being fully known and honest? How can we better experience this transparency, even now?

As you wrap up your time together as a group, challenge everyone to prayerfully seek a trusted person with whom they can be completely transparent, experiencing the freedom found in confessing sin and being fully known.

READ SESSION 3 AND COMPLETE THE PERSONAL STUDY BEFORE THE NEXT GROUP EXPERIENCE.

CONSIDER GOING DEEPER INTO THIS CONTENT BY READING CHAPTER 4 IN MATT CHANDLER AND MICHAEL SNETZER'S BOOK RECOVERING REDEMPTION (B&H, 2014).

THE RESPONSE: FAITH & REPENTANCE

Jesus said you'll know a tree by its fruit (see Luke 6:43-45). You can know what's inside you by the evidence your life is bearing.

The proof of Christianity isn't perfection. In fact, one of the key ways you can tell you're saved—as backward as this logic may feel or sound—is when your faith continually leads you toward repentance, and Jesus continually brings about change.

A Christian's ongoing response to the gospel is a steady stream of repentance. If apples on a limb identify an apple tree, so repentance is a fruit that reveals the inner essence of a person who trusts in Jesus Christ.

THE FRUIT OF FAITH

How do you know you've trusted in Christ for salvation?

Some people think they're Christians because they celebrate Christmas, maybe they attend church on Easter, and they don't practice another religion. Or because they were born in America. Or because they grew up going to church. Or because they were baptized as a kid. And they've been doing their best ever since, living a pretty good life, trying to be a moral person.

Our culture seems to be OK with calling ourselves Christians without any tangible, qualitative difference in our lives. But the Bible won't let us get away with calling ourselves Christians without the fruit of faith. So it's important (no matter how uncomfortable) to honestly evaluate our lives for the evidence of salvation.

READ ROMANS 3:9-26, BUT WHEN YOU COME TO THE WORDS JEW OR GREEK, SUBSTITUTE A WORD DESCRIBING THE RELIGIOUS HERITAGE YOU GREW UP IN OR ARE CURRENTLY A PART OF (BAPTIST, METHODIST, CATHOLIC, ETC.).

What thoughts came to your mind as you read the passage this way?

What does this passage say about the benefit of culture, personal effort, and the paths we wander down in seeking righteousness?

Now don't miss this. A lot of people want to believe repentance is outdated. They may think things like: *Repentance was an Old Testament thing for people under law—for prophets delivering bad news in sackcloth; we're living beyond the New Testament in grace now, right? Guys like John the Baptist came in camel skins and leather, eating bugs in the wilderness until he got his head cut off, but Jesus changed all that, sprinkling love dust on everyone, telling us to forget all that angry repentance stuff, right? Isn't that what Paul said there in Romans?* Let's remind ourselves of how Jesus introduced His ministry.

READ MARK 1:1-15.

What explicit similarities characterize John's and Jesus' ministries?

"Repent and believe" (v. 15) is much more than what happened when God first saved you. It's part of the ever-growing lifestyle of a Spirit-led believer.

In your own words explain your daily need for repentance.

"The time is fulfilled, and the kingdom of God is at hand" (v. 15) was the announcement that Jesus was the hope the prophets had been pointing toward. The message of repentance and belief hadn't changed. Christ made genuine transformation possible in the hearts of God's children.

Obviously, anybody can call themselves a Christian. They can want to be good, wish they were different, make any number of outside-in adjustments, and add religious activities to their schedules. But only a follower of Christ has been given what's needed to truly hate sin and desire true righteousness from the inside out.

Have you ever heard someone say, "I know he's a Christian; he just isn't living like it"? On what is that claim of Christian identity based (baptism, prayer, upbringing, etc.)?

Based on what you've seen in Scripture, what does Jesus say about faith and a life that doesn't bear the fruit of repentance?

READ 1 JOHN 1:5-10.

What specific areas call for repentance in your life today?

Name specific ways your life has been—and is being—transformed. If you can't honestly identify any evidence of salvation, what does this lack of fruit suggest?

True faith produces repentance. It's a necessary part of growing into maturity and a sure sign that we've been born again in genuine faith. It shows that God is at work in us from the roots up. Repentance is the living fruit of redemption.

So contrary to the way it may feel, with our natural leaning toward performance-based validation and perfectionism, continual repentance can be a good and healthy thing.

But this is where it gets tricky—and here's where doubts can start rolling in—because we probably know by now that we're pretty good at faking repentance when we need to. We can feel sorry and not really change. And so if the fruit of faith is repentance and if our only way to change what's wrong with us is by trusting Jesus, then how can we tell if our repentance is real—the kind that truly leads to change?

We'll begin to answer that question in the following pages.

AS YOU PRAY, ASK GOD TO REVEAL TO YOU THE FRUIT OF YOUR FAITH (OR LACK THEREOF). THIS REQUEST TAKES SURRENDER AND HUMILITY. ASK, "HAVE I PUT MY FAITH COMPLETELY IN YOU?" AND LISTEN FOR HIS REPLY.

3.2

WORLDLY GRIEF

OK, so you've done it again. You know, the sin that so easily entangles you. Put yourself there for a second. Sit back and feel it. Sad is an understatement. You're equal parts ashamed, angry, frustrated, discouraged, shocked, remorseful, depressed. You're a lot of things. And none of them are happy.

You feel terrible about it. Really, you do.

The Bible calls this terrible feeling *grief*—a word we commonly apply to the deep feelings of loss experienced with the death of a loved one. But *grief* is also a fitting term to describe what happens in the aftermath of sin. Of all the things our sin leaves us with, one of the most significant is a deep measure of loss.

READ 2 CORINTHIANS 7:8–10.

> In your own words compare and contrast the two kinds of grief and what each produces.

Godly Grief	Worldly Grief

> What did you learn from the video teaching and group discussion about this Scripture?

Worldly grief tends to be the norm for most people, Christians and non-Christians. To better understand worldly grief, let's look at four death-inducing grief responses. Then humbly and honestly consider how you usually respond to your sin. As you diagnose personal ways of exhibiting grief, prayerfully consider how God and even how others would describe your attitude toward sin.

HORIZONTAL GRIEF

Horizontal repentance is less concerned about being broken and more upset about getting busted. It's sorry for the consequences being suffered, not necessarily what was done. Honestly, if you hadn't been caught, you might still be doing it. And if you could do it again without getting caught, you would be more careful next time.

Could there be some weepy, "I'm sorry" promises coming from these events? Sure. Could you really be sorry for how your family, coworkers, or others now see you? Absolutely. But tissues and tears don't tell the whole story. What's missing from this picture is any view of God—a vertical perspective. There's no understanding that sin is bad not only because the horizontal consequences sting but also because it's poison.

When you hurt another person, is your grief strictly for horizontal consequences—"I'm sorry someone busted me"—or does it also include a vertical dimension—"I'm broken and, before God and the person I hurt, I'm truly sorry"?

Are you honestly more sorry for what you've done or the consequences?

How have you experienced horizontal grief over consequences that didn't ultimately lead to a change in behavior?

EMOTIONAL GRIEF

Maybe you didn't get caught, but the weight of your guilt is crushing. You're desperate never to feel this way again. You hate it. It makes you sick. You can't believe what just happened. Again. All the crying and carrying on make for dramatic and sincere sounding confessions. But raw emotions don't lead to repentance. Emotions change; they're driven by circumstances. So once the show is over and the aspirin has started to kick in, those feelings—the ones that made all those heartfelt promises—are nowhere to be found, no matter how much you seemed to mean it when you said it.

What emotional promises have you made about secret sin?

Does your grief tend to come from impulses? Once your emotions settle down, do you go right back to what you were doing?

How can you tell whether your sorrow is driven by emotional zeal alone or by a spiritual motivation?

PASSIVE GRIEF

We think if we just watch our sin more carefully, we can keep it under control. No problem. It won't happen again. If we just manage it a little better, we'll be fine. No need to overreact. We believe we can train our sin the way we can train a dog. But sin is more like a lion. It's wild and can't be tamed.

Worldly sorrow isn't serious about killing sin. It's passive. It says, "Man, I can't believe that happened. You sit! Bad lion!" We do this in hopes the lion won't maul us later as we show it who's boss. Worldly sorrow doesn't see the danger we're in with sin. It's playing with forces that are monumentally more powerful than we are, all the while believing we can hold it in check. Simply put, passive grief doesn't want to bother with getting rid of sin; it may even kind of like the sin hanging around.

When have you been surprised by the pain of sin?

What specific ways have you tried to train sin, hoping it wouldn't rear its ugly head?

What lions are you allowing to hang around that are continually biting you or will bite you if you don't put them to death?

IRRESPONSIBLE GRIEF

Worldly grief often sounds like "I'm sorry if …" or "I'm sorry you …" It's the kind of apology you hear athletes, celebrities, and politicians offer in the media: "I'm sorry that offended you." That's not an apology! The problem has been made out to be the response—presumably the mistaken response, not the action. This kind of grief is full of pride and avoids responsibilities and consequences. Blame has been shifted and the burden put on someone or something else.

You're not necessarily saying you did the right thing. But none of this would have happened if your spouse wouldn't spend so much money, if your kids would respect your authority, if your job wasn't so stressful, if … You feel misunderstood at best, and at worst, you feel like a victim.

Which of these do you tend to say: "I'm sorry you …" or "I'm sorry I …"?

What excuses do you make to avoid responsibility for your sin?

How does passing the blame for your actions, even the ones you feel sorry for, keep you trapped?

It's important to recognize that these four worldly ways of handling grief aren't exclusive to non-Christians. Even as believers, we can easily adopt worldly expressions of grief. It's part of human nature. But here's the thing: we'll needlessly spin our wheels every time we operate in one of these gears. Nothing will change. We'll never move on or get out of the rut we're stuck in. We simply won't arrive at the freedom found in true repentance when we're fueled by worldly grief.

We'll be people who carry around the opportunity for regret-free living yet never get traction because we'd rather protect our image and treat sin as if it's no big deal.

But it is. It's bad. It's deadly.

And the sooner we realize this, the sooner we can start experiencing the freedom of redemption and true confidence in our relationship with Christ. If we believe He's saved us, it's time to start living as though the sin for which He endured the cross was a big deal. It's time to start living out who we really are—the people Jesus died to redeem—instead of projecting a sanitized self-image to the world.

AS YOU CLOSE IN PRAYER, ASK GOD TO HELP YOU MOVE FROM WORLDLY SORROW TO GODLY SORROW, THE SORROW THAT LEADS TO REAL REPENTANCE, WHICH LEADS YOU TO A KNOWLEDGE OF THE TRUTH AND REAL CHANGE.

GODLY GRIEF

Rather than feeling the need to look invincible, pretending to be people we're not—or rather than giving up on ourselves altogether, convinced of how disappointed God must be in us—let's finally trust God's redemption.

But a redeemed life still experiences pain. Don't ever despise the pain points. Don't ignore them. Don't numb them. Pay attention. Grief felt over sin and weakness still present in our lives may actually be God at work. It could be instrumental in a valuable diagnosis, pinpointing deeper issues, and putting us on the road to healing.

Trusting God brings change. Faith manifests itself in repentance. It turns us around from our old, crooked paths to follow His way. It's the decisive shift not only in our thoughts, feelings, and actions but also in the overarching trajectory of our lives. In this final part of session 3, we'll examine the progression of godly grief.

GODLY GRIEF HAS CLEAR VISION

Worldly grief is horizontal, blind to the deep roots of sin and vertical offense against God. On the other hand, godly grief has sight. And even though seeing our sin in all its horror can be a painful experience, may we never overlook the divine mercy of God stripping off the blinders and giving us clarity to recognize sin for what it is.

READ LUKE 15:11-24.

What did it take for the son to see his sin?

What was the son's response to his sin? How did the father's response surprise the son?

How is your story like the prodigal son's?

READ HEBREWS 4:12-13.

How has God's Word helped you see what's in your heart? How has it revealed your rebellious ways? Be specific.

God's Word is surgical. It cuts deep. And it hurts when we're laid open. But the wisdom guiding the operation leads to recovery and healing. That deep-rooted, festering cancer is being removed from our hearts, where it was choking the life out of us. Let Him show you what He sees.

GODLY GRIEF PRODUCES SORROW
When the Bible described men and women seeing their sin before God—when He opened their eyes spiritually—they were appalled, horrified, grief-stricken. They felt an embitterment of the soul. That's the proper response to sin.

READ LUKE 7:36-50.

How did this woman respond to Jesus?

How did the Pharisee respond to her and to Jesus?

How did Jesus respond to her?

In what ways can you relate to this woman? To this Pharisee?

GODLY GRIEF READILY CONFESSES

After gaining sight for your sin and experiencing sorrow, the worst thing you can do is to hide your sin, hoping nobody ever finds out who you really are. You can be enslaved by the fear that someone will discover the sin you have genuine sorrow over. The best way to avoid being found out is to put everything out in the open. Be open with people about your struggles. Be open in your praise of God for what He's making of you, despite your many messes and problems. How crazy is it to admit that none of us are perfect yet spend so much time hiding the fact that we're not perfect?

Even if you're 99 percent known, you're still unknown. You're still hiding. You're still covering up. You're still giving sin and shame a dark place to hide, grow, and resurface.

True sorrow over sin begs to be vented—both vertically to God and horizontally to others. So mark this down: you have no shot at experiencing real freedom, change, and love if you're habitually protecting your image and pretending you're perfect. Maybe you'll confess sins with minimal collateral damage socially—something like coveting or not praying often enough. But you never drop the bomb that you struggle with something people deem more serious. Do you see how even what you confess can get twisted into a form of pride? And even the smallest bit of hiding closes you off from the blessings of being fully known. That 1 percent you're hiding will justify the voice of self-hatred, abusing you with whispers in your head: *Of course they love you, they don't know about ... If they knew, they wouldn't love you. You're unlovable.*

READ PSALM 32:5 AND JAMES 5:16.

> With whom are you 100 percent honest? If you don't have at least one person, ask God to show you a person with whom you can be honest.

> What are you still trying to hide? What will you do to shed your mask and be fully known?

Don't shortcut this step! There's no way around it.

Right now a lie is coming from the shadows of your heart, insisting you don't need to confess *that*. God promised that prayerfully confessing your sin is a necessary step toward healing and freedom. You can never walk in the light of His grace with one foot standing in a dark corner. Trust Him. (You may want to reread 1 John 1:5-10.)

GODLY GRIEF LEADS TO ACTION

Remember the lion tamer from our look at passive responses? Godly grief doesn't justify the lion's presence anymore. It stops fooling around with trying to train it. It doesn't buy it a kennel, a new chew toy, or a leash. It drags it out and puts it to death by the power of the Holy Spirit. Honestly, some lions are going to require that we pull the trigger multiple times, maybe even over the course of decades.

It can't be said enough. Don't try to pacify the sorrow or numb the symptoms. Godly grief allows pain to have its full and desired effect, alerting us to danger and areas of sickness so that they can be dealt with. Sin will kill or be killed. Cut it out of your life.

READ LUKE 19:1-10.

This isn't a formula for precise restitution. Like the woman with the perfume in Luke 7, the extreme response of Zacchaeus is a picture of godly grief and active repentance. We see a reversal of the attitude toward sin that had characterized his life before he experienced the grace of Jesus.

> Not to prove sincerity or earn forgiveness but out of the gratitude that overflows from a transformed heart, what specific action will you take to deal with sin and move in a new direction?

GODLY GRIEF PRODUCES SHAME

But wait; isn't shame bad? There's a worldly kind of shame that puts you in a tailspin, a downward spiral of shame-based behavior. It lures you into going back down the same path that led you into shame, in an effort to escape your discomfort or disgust. You can't believe you did that, drank that, looked at that, so you feel ashamed. Then you seek relief from the pain by numbing it with even more food, sex, pornography, drugs, busyness, or whatever it was that first brought on the feelings of shame. (You'll look at this cycle more specifically in session 6.)

But submitting ourselves to a Father's loving hand has a good weight. As a child of the King, you feel ashamed for rebelling against His goodness, for seeking satisfaction apart from life with Him. Instead of pressing you even lower into yourself and deeper into sin, the stern hand of God propels you forward, stuns you back to sensibility, and points you back up to your Creator. This godly shame is a deep regret that steers you out of sin and back toward the path leading to life.

READ PSALM 3:1-3.

> Have you ever felt there was no salvation for your soul? Imagine God coming to you in your shame, bending down, placing His holy hands under your chin, raising your eyes to meet His, and then gently lifting up your head and calling you back toward the life He has for you. What's your response as He lifts up your head and calls you back to Him?

Christ bore the shame of the cross—the shame you deserve—and took it on Himself. He died for your sin and was raised to new life, to the glory of God. You've been set free from the burden of sin and its shame. Godly grief drives you to the feet of Jesus. Repentance is just a sweet surrender, a giving of yourself over to your Creator and Redeemer, trusting Him with your life—all of it.

THANK JESUS FOR "DESPISING THE SHAME" WHEN HE WENT TO THE CROSS AND DIED FOR YOU (HEB. 12:2). ASK GOD FOR HIS POWER TO DO WHAT ONLY HE CAN DO IN LEADING YOU TO REPENTANCE. ASK THE HOLY SPIRIT TO CONVICT YOU OF SIN. FINALLY, CELEBRATE YOUR REDEMPTION. CELEBRATE YOUR REDEEMER. CELEBRATE AS THE PRODIGAL SON CELEBRATED WITH HIS FATHER!

THE RESULT: JUSTIFICATION & ADOPTION

BEGIN YOUR DISCUSSION WITH THE ACTIVITY BELOW.

In the previous session you were encouraged to pray about finding a trusted person and meeting to confess sin and be fully known. How did that go?

In what ways did you sense the Holy Spirit working on you as you dug into Scripture about repentance during your personal study of session 3?

What did you learn specifically about the fruit of faith? About worldly grief and false repentance, compared to godly grief and true repentance?

We've laid important groundwork so far with the reality of our sinfulness; our only hope being found in the remedy of the gospel; and what it means to respond with genuine, saving faith as evidenced by repentance. The final piece of this foundation is what that all means at the core of who we are. If the heart of the problem is the problem of the heart, then what transformation happens at the heart level? We can't just change our behavior. The gospel recovers our relationship with God and redeems our identity.

TO PREPARE FOR THE VIDEO, READ ALOUD EPHESIANS 1:3-9:

Blessed be the God and Father of our Lord Jesus Christ, who has blessed us in Christ with every spiritual blessing in the heavenly places, even as he chose us in him before the foundation of the world, that we should be holy and blameless before him. In love he predestined us for adoption as sons through Jesus Christ, according to the purpose of his will, to the praise of his glorious grace, with which he has blessed us in the Beloved. In him we have redemption through his blood, the forgiveness of our trespasses, according to the riches of his grace, which he lavished upon us, in all wisdom and insight making known to us the mystery of his will, according to his purpose, which he set forth in Christ.

WATCH

COMPLETE THE VIEWER GUIDE BELOW AS YOU WATCH SESSION 4.

To be justified is to be found _____, to be made _____.

You and I have been justified before God. The sovereign Judge of the universe has banged the gavel and declared us _____.

You don't just have a Judge, but you have a loving _____.

The moment you are justified, you're also _____. They happen simultaneously.

When the Judge adopts you, you have the freedom not to give in to the _____ you experienced before your justification and adoption.

All we do to be justified and delighted in by God, to be declared innocent and loved as sons and daughters, is simply by faith _____ God has done what He said He was going to do in Jesus Christ.

WAYS THE SPIRIT TESTIFIES TO OUR SPIRIT THAT WE ARE CHILDREN OF GOD

1. There is an acknowledgment of the _____ of Christ.
   We have a desire for _____, although it is imperfectly executed.

2. There is joy in our _____ as we imperfectly execute obedience.
   There's a _____ of the things of the Lord.

We get God: unfettered, unbroken, complete access to our _____ and what our soul was designed to experience.

The call to follow Jesus Christ is also a call to _____.
The sovereign King of glory will use the dark night to _____ our souls to Him.

You have a loving Father, and you have His _____. You have not been abandoned.

Your Father _____ in you—not a better version of you but you.

Video sessions available for purchase
at *www.lifeway.com/recoveringredemption*

DISCUSS THE VIDEO SEGMENT, USING THE QUESTIONS BELOW.

What stood out to you in this message?

Matt spoke of justification in legal terms. How would you describe what it means for a Christian to be justified? (See Gal. 2:16.)

If you are an adopted child of God …

How does that affect your identity?

What privileges does that bestow to you?

What responsibilities come along with the family name?

How have you wrestled with the doctrines of justification or adoption applying to you? How might you believe them theologically but struggle to experience them practically?

Romans 8:15 says you "did not receive the spirit of slavery to fall back into fear, but you have received the Spirit of adoption as sons, by whom we cry, 'Abba! Father!'" So as Christ-followers, we're no longer enslaved to *self*, *others*, *the world*, or *religion*.

Discuss how your identity as an adopted child of God frees you from the slavery of those four empty wells.

Matt said the Spirit testifies to our spirit that we are children of God (see Rom. 8:16) through a pursuit of the Lord, including both a desire for obedience to Christ and joy in our Father.

Describe this desire and joy you have as you pursue the things of God.

As you end your time together, pray, thanking God for both justification and adoption. Ask Him to help you embrace both of these life-changing realities.

READ SESSION 4 AND COMPLETE THE PERSONAL STUDY BEFORE THE NEXT GROUP EXPERIENCE.

CONSIDER GOING DEEPER INTO THIS CONTENT BY READING CHAPTER 5 IN MATT CHANDLER AND MICHAEL SNETZER'S BOOK RECOVERING REDEMPTION (B&H, 2014).

THE RESULT: JUSTIFICATION & ADOPTION

What God does for us in redemption seems to be literally unbelievable. But it's true.

It's incredible that He fully knows us yet loves us. When we realize that truth, how could it not define who we are and drive what we do?

Our relationship with God can't be managed like other things. It has to be the one factor that affects and wires everything else. God isn't something to be bolted onto our lives or worked into our busy schedule. He's our Creator and Redeemer, Judge and Father.

To really get our minds around that, we have to understand two theological terms—*justification* and *adoption*—that will lead us to a third. We'll study the third, *sanctification*, in the next session.

So if the heart of the problem is the problem of the heart, how does redemption transform us at the core of our being?

4.1

GOD THE JUDGE—JUSTIFICATION

Modern culture is obsessed with justice. Don't think so? Try turning on the TV without finding an episode of *Law & Order* or *CSI*. Producers have the golden ticket: set heinous crimes in different cities. That's all we want, apparently. Then there's actual legal drama that we've twisted into entertainment. Put the seemingly perfect neighbor on trial and good luck finding anything else to watch or read. News, sitcoms, TV dramas, movies—it doesn't matter—as long as it involves the legal system or an investigation.

We are a people ruled by law. We want fairness. We want the truth to come out. We want the innocent to be cleared and for somebody to pay.

We want justice.

And guess what? The gospel gives it to us.

> How do you see your desire for justice play out in daily life?

READ ROMANS 8:28-30.

> What do these verses teach about salvation? (Note the sequence of God's plan and work.)

> What do these verses teach you about God?

> About yourself?

Justification is a legal term. The biblical idea of justification means the gavel bangs down, and we're declared innocent. But how is this possible? How can a fair Judge declare us innocent? Isn't God everywhere all the time, so that nothing escapes His all-seeing notice? How in the world, then—based on the preponderance of evidence that could be displayed against us—could we get off with a not-guilty verdict? Have we slipped through on a technicality or something?

> What do you learn from the following verses about justification?
>
> Romans 5:8-9
>
> Galatians 2:15-16
>
> James 2:20-26
>
> What's the difference between basing your salvation on your own good works and having a faith that's active and alive, proving itself by works?
>
> What confidence and hope in God do these passages on justification give you?

As a result of the sacrifice and willing substitution of the innocent, crucified Christ, God has imputed to us—credited to us, ascribed to us, placed into our account—all the innocence and righteousness and perfection of Christ.

Therefore, a miserable end to our lives has been miraculously averted, literally. It's only by divine intervention. Not in theory or through roundabout scholarly logic. Not by spiritual delusion or false hopes. Not on the condition that we try to be extra careful from here on out. Not on any of that. On the cross. By the empty grave. In Christ.

READ COLOSSIANS 2:13-14.

> What do these verses say, definitively, about your guilt and your ability to repay any debt owed to God?

Christ paid our penalty—nailing the certificate of debt to the cross—and freed us from the legal consequences of our treason against the King. His crucifixion took the full weight of sin; put it to death, once and for all; and buried it in a tomb that's now empty.

His resurrection provides all the objective evidence we need that His promises are true, that sin is ultimately powerless over us, that His ability to conquer death is real, and that His atonement is actively in force.

We've been justified before God. Declared innocent. Count on it.

> Reflect for a moment on the fact that Christ's innocence, righteousness, and perfection have been imputed to you, not based on what you've done but on what Jesus did. Write your thoughts as you meditate on this.

> If Jesus hadn't risen from the dead, would you have the same hope and assurance that you do now? Why or why not?

> How will these passages on justification shape your interactions with God this week?

AS YOU BEGIN TO PRAY, GO BACK TO THE QUESTION IN WHICH YOU REFLECTED ON CHRIST'S INNOCENCE, RIGHTEOUSNESS, AND PERFECTION BEING IMPUTED TO YOU. USE THE THOUGHTS AND WORDS YOU WROTE TO LEAD YOUR PRAISE TO GOD.

GOD THE FATHER—ADOPTION

The moment we were justified, something else was simultaneously taking place. We were not only declared innocent—legally—but also adopted—relationally. As the Judge's gavel hit the block, He was also stepping down to welcome us as Father. Both of these things, from a positional standpoint, were accomplished in a moment's time.

But from an experiential standpoint—the way it feels, the way we live it—most of us take years, maybe all our lives, before we can wrap our heads and hearts around this other aspect of redemption. It's one thing to see God as Judge and believe we get to go to heaven someday when we die. It's harder for us to believe God also delights in us now, as sons and daughters of our Heavenly Father. We've been given eternal and abundant life in Christ.

READ ROMANS 8:14-17.

> Write down any words or phrases from this passage that describe the new identity you've received.

> Use these two columns to reflect on what you didn't receive (although you may have deserved it on your own merit) and what you've received. Go beyond the words in this passage to include ways your life reflects these things practically. In other words, what would slavery look like in your life now, and what does being adopted look like for you?

Didn't Receive	Received

Describe ways you've grown in your understanding of justification and adoption.

In what areas of life do you struggle with the way God sees you—your position and identity before Him? Where do you find hope?

Why do you think Christians who believe they're justified wrestle with the fact that God really delights in them?

Because we've been justified and adopted, we've received new hearts, and those hearts are no longer locked in the enslavement of *self*, *others*, *world*, and *religion*. We aren't slaves to those things, whereas before justification and adoption we most definitely were.

Look back at the four wells we run to, hoping to fix ourselves or to feel better. Think about your group conversation and the video segment on these. Write ways your justification and adoption as a child of God help you see and respond differently to each of these.

Self:

Others:

The world:

Religion:

It's unbelievable.

God hasn't just given us the break we needed; He's given us the identity we needed.

He's not only the Judge; He's also our Father.

That's your identity—a child of God, of the heavenly King, of the Ruler over all, of the Judge of the whole earth. This sovereign and transcendent God has also chosen to be Father. Your Father.

READ GALATIANS 4:1-7.

What do you learn from this passage about your identity?

The apostle Paul was talking to spiritually immature believers ("children," v. 3) who were still trying to grow through legalistic means, which kept them enslaved. How have you seen legalism stunt spiritual growth?

How does legalism have an appearance of maturity while truly being evidence of immaturity?

How does your adoption as an heir help you grow to maturity in Christ?

READ GALATIANS 4:8-9.

Where do you catch yourself slipping back into old patterns—living like a slave instead of an adopted child, an heir with Christ?

Finally, because the truth of adoption is harder to experience in your heart than to accept in your mind, use the remaining space to write your thoughts and feelings about God delighting in you as a perfectly loving Father would delight in His son or daughter. Tell yourself that this great doctrine defines your new identity.

AS YOU CLOSE YOUR TIME WITH GOD IN PRAYER, BE STILL FOR SEVERAL MINUTES JUST LETTING THE REALITY SINK IN THAT GOD HAS ADOPTED YOU. HE'S CHOSEN YOU TO BE HIS CHILD IN HIS FAMILY. SIMPLY BE STILL AND KNOW THAT HE'S YOUR FATHER.

4.3

THE SPIRIT'S TESTIMONY

This is too important to miss. If it still feels too good to be true that God has not only declared you justified, removing your guilt, but also adopted, delighting in you, He speaks to you through His personal presence. Much like repentance can't be driven by emotion, justification and adoption can't be based on emotion. We can't trust emotion.

It's not about how you feel. It's about what He's done. He gave Himself *for* you in Christ and He gives Himself *to* you in His Spirit.

He has not only given you a new identity, but also His Spirit. And this Spirit of adoption "bears witness" that we're "children of God" (Rom. 8:16).

REREAD ROMANS 8:12-17.

> How would you describe the inner conviction from the Holy Spirit that
> you are God's child?

Now the courtroom scene is back in play. The expert witness is on the stand, but the plot twist is this: you're both the subject and the jury now. You're the one being testified about and the one who needs to be convinced of the truthfulness of this reality. Furthermore, this isn't some indifferent fact-checker; the Witness is also your personal Counselor. The very Spirit God has given to you as your Source of power and Teacher of truth is constantly bearing witness to this fact:

You belong to God.

We see this testimony play out in a couple of ways.

First, the Spirit testifies to our spirit that we're God's children when we acknowledge the lordship of Christ. We give our life to Him, surrender, and desire to be obedient.

What evidence is there that you desire to obey God, even if imperfectly?

How does that evidence testify that you're a child of God? (Or if no evidence is present, what does that testimony reveal?)

A second way the Spirit testifies to our spirit that we're God's children is that we have joy in that intimate relationship with Him, as we call Him, "Abba! Father!" (v. 15). Abba is a personal term going beyond mere legal status to relational honor and affection.

What evidence is there of joy in your personal relationship with God?

How does that joy testify that you're God's child?

None of us would dare to say, of course, that we follow God perfectly. We'll never be flawless in the execution. But is the desire there? Do we want it? Is our heart leaning in the direction of obedience and trust? If we could only get our stubborn will to line up with His will on a consistent basis, isn't that the way we'd want to go?

But the more we persevere in our pursuit of Him, the more clearly the Spirit will bear witness "with our spirit" (v. 16) that we truly belong to Him, that we're indeed the children of God.

READ PROVERBS 24:16 AND HEBREWS 12:1-2.

What hope do these verses give you?

What do they tell you about perfectionism in living out your faith?

This week, how will you continue pursuing God, even when you get entangled or fall on your face?

This is the only road leading to satisfaction, wholeness, acceptance, freedom, healing, and joy. No more crooked paths to empty wells. God has more for you. Stop settling.

One day our Father is going to redeem all creation; He's going to restore the peace that existed before sin entered the world. There'll be a new heaven. New earth. New bodies.

And better still—better even than giving us the body we've always wanted, living in a place more beautiful and perfect than we can possibly imagine—He's going to give us Himself. We'll be able to enjoy unbroken and unending fellowship with our strong Abba Father, which is a million times more precious and desirable than all His other blessings put together.

That's the inheritance for His children—for His heirs. And here's one more plot twist: an inheritance is shared after someone dies, but in this case we enjoy the riches of His inheritance and life with our resurrected Redeemer.

READ REVELATION 21:1-7; 22:1-7.

How do these passages describe the inheritance and future for all God's children? Write as many specific things as possible.

Why is unending access to the presence of God the true blessing?

Heirs of God. That's the very identity the gospel ascribes to us, "provided we suffer with him in order that we may also be glorified with him" (Rom. 8:17).

What good effect can suffering have in the spiritual growth of heirs with Christ?

READ JAMES 1:2-4.

How have you seen God at work lately in the various trials of your life?

The reason He can tell us to "count it all joy" when we meet "trials of various kinds" (v. 2)—which pretty much covers it all, wouldn't you say?—is that God does some of His best work amid our worst pain. Our senses are never more awakened to our need for His love than when we're most helplessly exposed. God isn't the author of this evil and suffering, but His power is great enough to turn the darkest nights into something beautifully redemptive for His children.

READ ROMANS 8:31-39.

What causes you to doubt God's love for you?

How does the entire chapter of Romans 8 encourage you? Specifically, how is the Spirit comforting you with the truths in this text?

If you belong to God, nothing can separate you from His love. Nothing. If you're His. He's the Creator of all but only the Father of those who've been justified and adopted. The Spirit testifies by putting a desire for and joy in obedience. Honestly, do you want to obey God? Do you find joy in obeying Him? Are you His child?

BEGIN YOUR PRAYER TIME BY THANKING YOUR HEAVENLY FATHER THAT HE ADOPTED YOU. ASK THE HOLY SPIRIT TO TESTIFY ON YOUR BEHALF THAT YOU'RE A CHILD OF GOD. THANK GOD FOR HIS DELIGHT IN YOU AND FOR THE TIMES OF SUFFERING HE USES TO BRING ABOUT SPIRITUAL GROWTH IN YOUR LIFE.

GROWING IN HOLINESS: SANCTIFICATION

BEGIN DISCUSSION WITH THE ACTIVITY BELOW.

What struck you in session 4 as you explored the doctrines of justification and adoption? What did you learn about God or about yourself?

How do you wrestle with the fact that we've been made right before a holy God, but our lives still don't always look holy?

When and how did you first become aware of the biblical concept of sanctification? Explain it in your own words.

We've now framed a full picture of what redemption is: the reality, the remedy, the response, and the result. But we know our lives don't always reflect this truth. We have positional holiness before God, but still wrestle with manifest holiness day-to-day. The doctrines of justification and adoption, which are instantaneous and simultaneous, lead us to a third theological term, *sanctification*, which is progressive and ongoing.

TO PREPARE FOR THE VIDEO, READ ALOUD PSALM 51:10-12:

> *Create in me a clean heart, O God,*
> *and renew a right spirit within me.*
> *Cast me not away from your presence,*
> *and take not your Holy Spirit from me.*
> *Restore to me the joy of your salvation,*
> *and uphold me with a willing spirit.*

WATCH

Positional holiness: when God looks at me, He sees me as spotless and _____.

God wants a manifest holiness, a _____ of our lives where our lives get more and more lined up with how He designed things to work, and we begin to look more and more like _____.

Sanctification requires grace-driven _____.

Vivification is a _____ of the Lord.

The first aspect of growing in visible holiness is setting our minds on the things that are _____ and getting our minds off the things that are _____.

You move toward functional holiness by the _____ of your mind.

Vivification is a training of the mind to think _____ about the Lord.

Mortification is putting to _____ what is sinful in you.

Sanctification is about _____ into the Lord, having our minds _____, and being very serious about putting anything to death that might either be sinful in Scripture or that might hinder my love for the Lord and my delight in the Lord.

HURDLES TO SANCTIFICATION

1. Treating _____
Treating symptoms most commonly reveals itself in _____ strife and conflict.

Treating symptoms reveals itself in _____.

If the _____ isn't changed, managing the behavior doesn't set anybody free.

Sanctification and going after the heart are God saying, "Son, Daughter, I have _____ for you than this."

2. _____ up
There should be, in and among the people of God, a _____ in our weaknesses.

Video sessions available for purchase
at *www.lifeway.com/recoveringredemption*

DISCUSS THE VIDEO SEGMENT, USING THE QUESTIONS BELOW.

What initial thoughts do you have? What did you learn or see anew?

Matt defined *sanctification* as "the ongoing transformation from one degree of glory to the next by the Holy Spirit of God, making you more and more like Jesus Christ." He said this requires "grace-driven effort," moving toward the things of the Lord.

What was your immediate response to the word *sanctification* before watching the video? How would you explain it now?

Two theological words were introduced, *vivification* and *mortification*. In your own words, what was meant by each (see Rom. 12:2; Col. 3:1-4)?

What specific ways have you personally practiced vivification? How is God's Word involved in giving you life?

Matt used his move to a new house as an example of renewing his mind. How have you developed a new spiritual habit until it became natural?

Colossians 3:5-10 lists some of the things we're called to put to death (mortify). When you feel that pull toward something that's clearly sinful, how do you usually handle it?

Matt talked about a couple of hurdles to our sanctification: our tendency to mow over the weeds—dealing with symptoms rather than matters of the heart—and covering up what's really going on in our hearts. Which of these do you tend toward most?

Before closing in prayer, ask: How can our small group help you in your process of sanctification? How can we encourage you in the renewal of your mind? How can we support you in mortifying what's sinful inside you?

READ SESSION 5 AND COMPLETE THE PERSONAL STUDY BEFORE THE NEXT GROUP EXPERIENCE.

CONSIDER GOING DEEPER INTO THIS CONTENT BY READING CHAPTER 6 IN MATT CHANDLER AND MICHAEL SNETZER'S BOOK RECOVERING REDEMPTION (B&H, 2014).

GROWING IN HOLINESS: SANCTIFICATION

Sanctification is learning to turn right where we used to turn wrong. It's a redirection—a reorienting of our lives.

There are two facets of holiness: *positional* holiness—standing blameless before God with the righteousness imputed to you by Christ—and *manifest* holiness—learning to walk upright as you take up your cross and follow Christ.

Honestly, this is often a two-steps-forward, one-step-back kind of stumbling along. But keep this in view: your Heavenly Father knows that growth is a process and He celebrates each step.

Justification and adoption were both God's work entirely. Sanctification— the visible, tangible, working out of that holiness—requires a joint effort on your part. Positional holiness is a moment of rebirth by God's grace; manifest holiness is a process of spiritual maturation, growing through the submission of your will to God's will.

Going in God's direction doesn't just happen by itself. It takes work. It takes sacrifice. It takes truly believing that what you'll find following His lead is more valuable and more satisfying than what was at the bottom of dry wells on dead-end paths.

God has more for you. Believe it. Don't settle for less. Keep going.

5.1

VIVIFICATION—PURSUING SPIRITUAL LIFE

Vivification. You probably haven't seen or used this word in a sentence lately—or ever—but it's one of three key words injected into your vocabulary through session 5. It basically means *to quicken or animate, to bring to life.*

You naturally move toward whatever you're focused on. It has gravity. If you're moving along in one direction, but staring over at something else, you start drifting off course.

Vivification is an intentional focus on godly things that leads you into abundant life. It involves filling ourselves with a renewed way of thinking, based on ultimate realities— things that stir up our love, gratitude, and affections for Jesus.

READ COLOSSIANS 3:1-4.

How would your life be different if you consistently kept your focus and attention on things above, where Christ is, rather than on earthly things?

Make a list of "things that are on earth" (v. 2) that capture your attention.

Make a list of specific "things that are above" (v. 2) to keep in view.

The Bible says you've been given the authority to monitor what you think about. So instead of believing lies, instead of nursing distortions, you can choose to dwell on the truths of the gospel, which you can be sure will always far transcend whatever is trending on social media this afternoon.

We're talking about thinking new stuff. True stuff. The mind is where vivification begins to build steam. By dwelling on what's eternally accurate about God and about ourselves, we're able to see that our lives are not uncontrollable, but they can be brought into alignment with truth. By the power of the Spirit, we can submit our lives, including our minds, to Christ—for our good and His glory.

READ ROMANS 12:2 AND 2 CORINTHIANS 10:5.

How do these two verses add to your understanding of vivification?

What does it look like, practically, to "take every thought captive to obey Christ" (2 Cor. 10:5)? When do you need to do that most?

In what areas or situations do you find it easiest to conform to the world?

READ JOHN 17:13-19.

What does Jesus say His followers are sanctified in (vv. 17-19)? And what's the result of the sanctification process (v. 13)?

Disciplined time in Scripture—reading, studying, memorizing—isn't legalism. It's smart. If you want to walk in the fullness of life, it makes sense that you train yourself to focus on Christ. Earlier in John 14:6 Jesus spoke of going to prepare a new home for His followers and said, "I am the way, and the truth, and the life. No one comes to the Father except through me."

The Word of God is essential to the daily, ongoing life of a believer. If God's message is not deep inside you, where you can meditate on it, return to it, and frequently call it back to mind, you won't be able to discern what's the true and right path from what may be an intriguing detour into this world that's no longer your home.

Taking charge of your mind, making sure your thoughts are pointing toward Jesus, is how you remember that your life has a new direction now.

READ HEBREWS 4:12.

In what ways can God's Word help you be transformed?

Do you believe the Bible is God's Word? Let that sink in—God's Word. If that's true, it isn't just a good book. It isn't just pages between covers or words on a screen. Do you believe your Creator, Redeemer, and Father has spoken and will keep speaking to you, His child? If you believe it's God's Word, are you passionately disciplined in spending time to know Him, hear Him, and focus the direction of your life on His way?

When do you spend intentional time with God's Word?

Slow down when you read the Bible. Put yourself into the story so that you can really feel who God is and understand that He will have the same grace for you as for those you read about. This is the kind of thing that fuels affection. It's a training of the mind to think rightly about the Lord, to understand where our new home is so that, out of habit, we don't make a wrong turn to an old house that's crumbling on the inside because it has no solid foundation. Focus on what builds up and brings life.

This is vivification.

READ PHILIPPIANS 4:8.

Write this verse as a final reminder of what vivification looks like.

CLOSE YOUR TIME TODAY IN PRAYER, THANKING GOD FOR LEADING YOU TO SPIRITUAL TRANSFORMATION, THE RENEWING OF YOUR MIND. ASK THE HOLY SPIRIT TO CONTINUE TO LEAD YOU AS YOU READ GOD'S WORD, AS YOU SET YOUR MIND ON HIM, AS HE RENEWS YOUR MIND.

MORTIFICATION—PUTTING THE FLESH TO DEATH

Some things just go together. They're inseparable.

This is the case with vivification and mortification. You can't do one without the other. Choosing to go one way is choosing not to go the other way. Sanctification requires both—pursuing spiritual life and putting the flesh to death. Putting on the new requires taking off the old.

READ COLOSSIANS 3:1-10.

> How are vivification and mortification related? Notice the word *therefore* in verse 5 as Paul described vivification (vv. 1-4) and then mortification (vv. 5-10). What's the motivation behind mortification?

> There are two sets of sins mentioned in this passage: those in verse 5 and those in verses 8-9. What are the differences between these two lists?

> Is one set of sins more serious than the other? Explain your answer.

Remember, there are things that just need to be dealt with, those untamable lions that need to be dragged into the light and put to death. When it comes to how we treat sin encroaching on our spiritual freedom, our tendency is to be way too accommodating with it—and to feel way too confident in our own ability to keep it in check.

> If someone looked at your life, would there be any sins you justify and tolerate as harmless, or could they say you believe the only acceptable sin is a dead sin?

Make a vertical list below of the sins mentioned in Colossians 3:5-9.

Then prayerfully ask the Holy Spirit to bring conviction about any of these sins in your life. In the space to the right, write thoughts, action steps, or prayers about mortifying these sins.

READ JOHN 16:5-15.

In your own words, explain the Spirit's role in the sanctification process.

Now some things are black and white. The Bible can be super specific. At times we may honestly wish it weren't so clear on certain issues. Other things fall into gray areas.

As you keep maturing in the faith and growing deeper in the sanctification process, God's Spirit will alert you to certain things that, even though they're not morally wrong, are detrimental to your heart and need to be cut out.

There's no Bible verse, for example, that prohibits sleeping until 10:00 on a Saturday morning, killing time with video games or social media, or listening to music from your wilder days. But for whatever reason—for you—there's a noticeable drag on your zeal for Christ when these things are present in your life. These things create resistance and drift, causing you to veer off course or, at best, slow down in your pursuit of God.

Maybe you start to see a connection between a specific activity that isn't addressed and a general characteristic that's described in Scripture. Maybe it's a common grace that, for personal reasons, stirs up your desire to indulge too deeply, distracting you from the Giver of the gift. Maybe there's someone who needs the hope you've found in Christ, but you're too busy to notice or ever cross that person's path. Maybe God just has something better for you, and this morally neutral thing is in its place.

Like it or not, there are some moral absolutes and universal truths.

Like it or not, there are also some things that are relative. They may not be inherently wrong for everyone, but they aren't healthy or helpful for you.

It takes maturity to discern and to personally deal with these issues that are relative. Immaturity either wants to make something wrong for everyone (a form of the legalism we explored previously) or justifies it and settles for stunted personal growth (a passive response to conviction). Vivification and mortification delve into even the gray areas in order to grow in sanctification and experience God's best.

READ PSALM 139:23-24 (READ THE WHOLE CHAPTER IF YOU HAVE TIME).

What sin in your life is Scripture absolutely clear about—even if it wasn't listed previously in Colossians 3? Write any specific Scriptures you may know that address sin you're wrestling with.

What things come to your mind that aren't morally wrong or prohibited in Scripture as sinful but are detrimental to your vitality and spiritual growth? In other words, what things may not be wrong but drain your focus, time, and energy?

If you need help determining gray areas, did anything immediately come to mind, but your natural response was, *What's wrong with that?* or *Where in the Bible does it say I can't do that?* Remember, the point is not whether you can do these things; the point is whether there's more joy for you in Christ without them.

What steps will you take to put these gray things to death?

How does putting to death the things of your earthly nature help you more diligently pursue the Lord?

Unlike the instantaneous gifts of justification and adoption, which were automatically deposited all at once into your account, sanctification requires a maturation period.

This growth process is a continual shifting of focus from the old to the new. From death to life. From earthly to spiritual.

You simultaneously choose not to turn left but instead to turn right to where you now live. You simultaneously choose not to feed that old desire but rather this new one. You put one to death and walk away from it. You pursue what brings new life.

Vivification. Mortification. They're literally a matter of life and death.

BEGIN YOUR TIME IN PRAYER BY ADMITTING YOUR POWERLESSNESS OVER SIN AND YOUR NEED FOR GOD TO EMPOWER YOU TO CONTINUALLY SEEK HIM, TO RENEW YOUR MIND, AND TO PUT TO DEATH THE SINFUL NATURE INSIDE YOU.

5.3

HURDLES TO SANCTIFICATION

There are hurdles to sanctification. This isn't an easy race.

Scripture repeatedly encourages Christ-followers to endure and persevere. So it's not a sprint to perfection. In fact, there's no finish line in this world. We can always take another step closer to God. That's why it's so foolish to pretend that we've arrived, that we're perfect, and then stumble over the hurdles we're about to knock down.

The most common barrier we bump up against in our process of sanctification is mowing over sin.

What makes this the hardest hurdle to get over is that it feels like the right approach. You're dealing with things you don't want in your life. But rather than dealing with heart issues, you identify symptoms and treat those exclusively rather than killing the root. Something ugly pops up. Attack it. Keep everything under control. Things look better on the surface. There may be virtually no trace left of that ugly patch in your life. "Congratulations," people may say. What a change … in appearance.

If all you do is mow over weeds, your work is only going to get harder. You'll constantly be cutting things down, and those weeds will pop up in new places, spreading like wildfire, choking out the good life. Just because you're constantly working to keep things trimmed neatly doesn't mean anything is healthy. And eventually that'll catch up to you, ruining everything.

Mowing over problems most often occurs in the fields of relationships and addictions. Let's deal with relationships first.

> Think about a difficult relationship that's causing you major headaches and anger. Write the name(s) of the person(s) below.

The easiest thing to do when you start locking horns with another person is to bail. Write them off. Don't answer their calls or texts anymore. Go to a different church. Find a new set of friends. Maybe even a new spouse. But in most cases, while you're fixated on what others have done to hurt or offend you, you're not seeing the need to dig up any roots in your own life. You're mowing over the real issue.

Conflict, by definition, requires two opposing forces.

So, by definition, any conflict you're having with others isn't entirely their fault. You're one of those opposing forces.

> When it comes to relational conflict, do you focus on the other person's flaws and weaknesses? How do you recognize your own contribution to the conflict?

Think back over the people you've spent the most time with over the years. Pay attention to the degree of consistency or turn-over. Do you tend to cut relationships off after a short while? Have you skipped around to different small groups or different churches? Have you bounced in and out of relationships? Are you always in the middle of drama? Do you often feel betrayed? Do you constantly feel unappreciated? Prayerfully consider whether your relational issues are a problem of your heart.

READ ROMANS 12:3 AND PHILIPPIANS 2:3.

> What principle do you see here for sanctifying your relationships?

READ COLOSSIANS 3:12-14 .

> What sanctified character traits cut out the roots of conflict?

Another area where we're prone to mow over the problem is addictive behavior and recurring sin. We're desperate to do whatever we can to stop the behavior. And that's certainly a wise first step in the right direction. But if we treat only the surface issues and evident symptoms without digging in to figure out what's actually spawning the pain from deep inside—even if we successfully rid ourselves of whatever that behavior was—we just trade one thing for another. We swap one thing we hate for another one we can tolerate—for a while. But it'll just be a new weed growing from the same root. And we still won't be free.

What recurring struggle have you been mowing over? How have you seen the root continually pop up in the same way or in new ways?

God wants you free forever from this addiction. What step will you take today to get to the root of the problem?

READ JEREMIAH 6:14.

Covering up is a second hurdle slowing down the progress of your sanctification. It's putting a bandage on a mortal wound. This is the "I'm fine" approach.

It's easy to tell yourself that someone is just being polite when they ask how you're doing, but do you ever open up? Is "Good" or "Blessed" always your answer? Are you deflecting, pretending, and covering up the pain points in your life?

When the fellow believers in your life check on you, asking probing questions to see how you've been applying the promises of God to your most troubling sin areas, you shouldn't feel busted and intruded on. No, it's a regular, encouraging reminder from God, spoken through the caring voice of friends, that He's fighting your battles on all fronts. He's right there with you, doing whatever it takes to strengthen and heal you, giving you the will and ability to obey.

Covering up is just dumb. Remember Adam and Eve trying to hide their shameful nakedness before the all-seeing Creator of the universe? We still think fig leaves and trees will do the trick. We mask ourselves with smiling faces and church vocabulary. You're not gaining a thing by covering it up, except keeping yourself enslaved to your secrets. And if you're being honest with yourself, you know this is true. Do you struggle with sexual immorality? Then confess it. With anger? Confess it. With lust? Just go ahead and confess it. With embarrassing addictions? Yes. Get it out there. The best way to start stripping sin of its power is to drag that dark beast into the light. How could that be any worse than what it's already done and is still doing to you?

READ PSALM 32:3-4.

What are the real results of covering up or pretending you're something you're not?

Is your small group a place where you feel you can be your true self, without covering up or pretending? Why or why not?

Are there any barriers, such as mistrust or broken confidentialities that keep you from completely opening up with your group? Write any of these barriers below.

How can the idea of sanctification—the fact that none of us are there yet, we're all still growing and becoming, we're all still learning how to live out the gospel—help you be honest and vulnerable with your group?

ASK FOR GOD'S POWER TO STOP MOWING OVER AND COVERING UP IN YOUR PROCESS OF TRANSFORMATION. USE PSALM 139 AS A GUIDE FOR YOUR PRAYER TO BE FULLY KNOWN.

KNOWING OUR BROKENNESS: FREE FROM SHAME

BEGIN DISCUSSION WITH THE ACTIVITY BELOW.

What was most helpful in your personal study of session 5? How did you see sanctification with fresh eyes?

Explain and give examples of vivification and mortification.

Toward the end of the previous personal study, you were asked several questions about our group—whether it's a safe place to be real. Would anyone like to share what you wrote or thought about? (This is a good time not to cover up!)

For the next several sessions we'll dig deeper into specific, practical examples of our sanctification. We'll start by examining how to break free from two unhealthy cycles, and then we'll look at developing healthy growth in our lives. The next step toward gospel freedom is a step we take together—being fully known.

TO PREPARE FOR THE VIDEO, READ ALOUD PSALM 25:1-11:

To you, O LORD, I lift up my soul.
O my God, in you I trust;
let me not be put to shame;
let not my enemies exult over me.
Indeed, none who wait for you shall be put to shame;
they shall be ashamed who are wantonly treacherous.
Make me to know your ways, O LORD;
teach me your paths.
Lead me in your truth and teach me,
for you are the God of my salvation;
for you I wait all the day long.
Remember your mercy, O LORD, and your steadfast love,
for they have been from of old.
Remember not the sins of my youth or my transgressions;
according to your steadfast love remember me,
for the sake of your goodness, O LORD! ...
For your name's sake, O LORD, pardon my guilt, for it is great.

WATCH

COMPLETE THE VIEWER GUIDE BELOW AS YOU WATCH SESSION 6.

Guilt is a falling of a clear moral _____. Shame has more to do with how we _____ ourselves and how we fall _____ of how we see ourselves.

HOW GUILT AND SHAME INTERACT

1. The most healthy way guilt and shame interact is when they _____ together: I might tell a lie and immediately feel guilty because I know lying is _____ but also feel shame because I think I'm _____ than that.

2. Guilt and shame can function _____ from one another: I can know I've done something morally wrong and not feel any _____ at all.

3. Guilt and shame can work _____ one another: we can feel shame for doing the _____ thing, and we can have a sense of glory in doing the _____ thing.

There is nothing more _____ _____ than loving and serving and having your life shaped by the Creator God of the universe.

If you're going to believe what the Bible says, but your self-ideal has been built around heroes in the _____, you have set yourself up for guilt and shame.

When you walk in guilt and shame, a by-product of that is oftentimes _____.

When self-hate exists, you will first _____ yourself.

There are times that self-hate begins to roll out onto _____.

You're not _____. So _____ are you before the King of glory that Christ died on the cross in your stead.

Nothing drives shame away from the heart more than being fully known yet still _____ in.

Justification takes care of our _____. Adoption takes care of our _____. Sanctification is the deconstruction of false self-ideals and a replacement of what is _____ and _____ and _____.

Our ideal, our picture, our model is _____ _____.

Video sessions available for purchase at *www.lifeway.com/recoveringredemption*

DISCUSS THE VIDEO SEGMENT, USING THE QUESTIONS BELOW.

Matt mentioned three ways guilt and shame interact, listed below. What examples of each one have you experienced?

1. Healthy: they work together—acknowledging guilt and feeling shame for it, which reveals something has gone wrong in the heart.

2. Unhealthy: they function independently of each other—doing something morally wrong and feeling no shame.

3. Unhealthy: they work against each other—feeling shame for doing the right thing and feeling glory in doing the wrong thing.

Matt referred to the cycle of guilt and shame as the perfect storm. How have you seen this wild destruction play out in your life?

The three doctrines unpacked earlier provide refuge from this perfect storm.

Justification. What does the Judge's declaration of "not guilty" do to the downward spiral of guilt and shame?

Adoption. Matt said nothing drives shame away from the heart more than being fully known yet still delighted in. How have you found that to be true in your life?

Sanctification. Becoming more like Jesus Christ deconstructs our false self-ideals and replaces them with what's true and right and good. The cycle of grace—grace feeds passion, which feeds grace, which feeds more passion—replaces the cycle of guilt and shame. (This doesn't mean we don't sin; it just means we fall back on grace rather than into shame when we do.) How do you see this cycle of grace working in your life?

Wrap up your group time in prayer, thanking God for leading His children out of the destructive storms of guilt and shame.

READ SESSION 6 AND COMPLETE THE PERSONAL STUDY BEFORE THE NEXT GROUP EXPERIENCE.

CONSIDER GOING DEEPER INTO THIS CONTENT BY READING CHAPTER 7 IN MATT CHANDLER AND MICHAEL SNETZER'S BOOK RECOVERING REDEMPTION *(B&H, 2014).*

KNOWING OUR BROKENNESS: FREE FROM SHAME

The created order disintegrated. Innocence gave way to guilt. Honor was replaced with shame.

We've all been born into this brokenness. And just like Adam and Eve, way back in the garden of Genesis 3, we've all tried to hide, covering up our guilt and shame. How absurd is it to believe we can hide from our Creator? How crazy is it to hide from our only hope of recovering innocence and honor?

God justifies us, delights in adopting us, and then leads us into the light of freedom through sanctification.

The only way out of this dark, downward spiral of guilt and shame is to be fully known.

We have to be honest with ourselves.

We have to be vulnerable before others.

We have to surrender to our Redeemer.

6.1

MEASURING UP—GUILT & SHAME

The incessant collision of guilt and shame thunders in our hearts, echoing louder each time we fall short of what we believe to be right and good. It can keep us awake at night and torture us throughout the day with its persistent pounding. This was certainly true of life before we were pulled out of the muck and mire—up from the pit of destruction. Unfortunately, this unhealthy cycle driving us deeper into shame can even be characteristic of people who've been justified and adopted by God.

How would life be different for you today if you could be completely vulnerable without any fear of rejection?

We often think of guilt and shame as if they're synonymous with each other. And even though they do (or should) overlap and interact with each other, they're not quite the same thing. Both indicate a failure in relation to a standard; however, guilt and shame are categorically distinct.

Finish these sentences, writing whatever comes into your mind.

I'm guilty of …

I feel ashamed because …

What differences do you see between guilt and shame?

Which is easier for you to recognize and try to correct? Why?

Guilt is experienced when we violate a clear moral code—a legality. *Shame* is experienced when we fail to measure up to an expectation—an identity.

In other words, guilt is more about what we do, and shame is more about who we are.

Psychologists say we all have a portrait in our minds of the person we'd like to be. They call this the self-ideal. When our lives don't reflect this image in our minds, we begin to feel shame.

The self-ideal we create for ourselves can incorporate a lot of expectations that simply aren't included in God's design for us. We can exalt the wrong kind of perfection. We can select the wrong kinds of heroes. We can decide that the touched-up look of magazine covers, the perks of a certain tax bracket, the personality of our old college roommate, or the filtered experiences shared through social media represent the life we should be living and the image we should be projecting.

> What's your self-ideal? Describe the hero in your mind that you'd like to believe is the real you if only other things would stop getting in the way.

> When your self-ideal doesn't show up in reality, how do you respond?

> When have you felt shame for something that wasn't wrong? What does that reveal about how you're defining your identity?

READ ROMANS 1:28-32.

> People can also be guilty of something and not feel any shame from it; they may even be proud of it. When have you experienced this?

What does experiencing guilt without shame reveal about the way you're defining your identity?

What's the difference between the guilt and shame associated with breaking a standard you've set in your mind and that which results from breaking God's glorious standards?

READ AMOS 7:7.

A plumb line is a clear and simple tool—a string drawn from one point to another—used to measure everything around it. Ultimately, we want our lives to line up with God's design. He's our Creator and Redeemer. Measuring ourselves by any other standard will result in deep roots of guilt and shame, throwing our lives out of order.

Like it or not, feelings of guilt and shame will help you see what standard you're elevating as supreme. Based on your examination in this session, by what are you measuring your identity?

What steps can you take to surrender areas that are out of line with who God says you are and how He's shown you to live?

TAKE TIME IN PRAYER TO CONFESS YOUR SINS. ADMIT YOUR GUILT BEFORE GOD, THE JUST JUDGE. ASK HIM TO WASH YOU CLEAN FROM YOUR SIN AND TO CLEANSE YOU OF YOUR GUILT. ACKNOWLEDGE THE SHAME YOU FEEL AND SURRENDER THAT TO HIM. ASK HIM TO CREATE A CLEAN HEART IN YOU. THANK HIM FOR HIS PRESENCE WITH YOU AND HIS LOVE FOR YOU.

6.2

THE PERFECT STORM—ANGER, ABUSE, & LUST

Guilt and shame don't exist in a vacuum. They stir up everything within you. And they feed one another. It's a seemingly inescapable loop.

The things we hate—things like anger, abuse, and lust—begin to resurface in our lives as all-too-familiar patterns of behavior. We hate them, but we don't seem to know any other way out of this shame we're drowning in.

Guilt leads to shame. Shame convinces us to do something we shouldn't. More guilt. More shame. More guilt. More shame. To say this is an unhealthy cycle is a wildly simplistic understatement; it's toxic.

> Describe the pain that your guilt-induced shame has caused you over the years.

> Describe shame-based behavior that has led you back into guilt.

The tension feeds a perfect storm, wreaking havoc in our lives, as we've already begun to see.

This usually starts with the surfacing of anger—something more along the lines of self-hate at first. We're kicking ourselves. Punishing ourselves. Does this sound familiar: *How many years has it been now? And I'm still not seeming to get any better at this. No stronger. No smarter. No further along. Weak and predictable. Just as everybody thinks. Just as everybody says. Just as everybody would see if they really knew everything … ?*

Let that frustration of guilt and shame keep building, and your heart becomes unable to hold it all in.

READ EPHESIANS 4:26-31.

Write some practical insights from this passage on how to uproot anger and break free from the cycle of shame.

What does it mean to give the Devil an opportunity (see v. 27)?

What specific opportunities are you allowing the devil because of anger?

READ PSALM 4.

Think about the last time you blew up in anger. Take a moment to ponder it in your heart, to search for the root cause. Write what comes to mind.

What hope does this psalm offer?

The pressure of anger builds and seeks an outlet in a couple of ways as we try to manage the tension between growing feelings of shame and a lowered sense of self-worth.

First, our anger turns inward; we feel worthless. So we begin treating ourselves cheaply, not taking care of our bodies and health, being reckless with habits, making it easier to be taken advantage of or looked down on.

Second (or simultaneously), the same insecurities can also express themselves as anger turned outward. We attack and tear down to gain control. If we can't be happy, then no one else deserves to be happy. If we can't feel good about ourselves, we'll make sure to give others good reasons not to feel good about themselves.

Anger has grown into abuse—abuse of others and abuse of ourselves.

We carelessly or even intentionally enter unhealthy situations and relationships. We turn against the people closest to us, abusing them with our quick-tempered mouths, physical aggression, or emotional manipulation.

Do you tend more toward self-abuse, the abuse of others, or both?

What are some recent examples?

An angry root grows into a toxic cycle of abuse. We were hurt, so we inflict more hurt.

This shame-based cycle of behavior also manifests itself in lust.

Abuse and lust both view others as objects to pacify our angry shame. With either pain or pleasure, we're seeking control of someone as a thing to be used. Our satisfaction comes at their expense. People become targets—outlets for pent-up shame and anger.

This dehumanization of others treats them as if they don't have souls, lives, or any other purpose in that moment other than to temporarily relieve our lustful craving or angry impulse.

In your own words, define dehumanization and explain how lust and abuse of any kind dehumanizes others.

Honestly, how have you dehumanized and objectified others for your own impulses, even if only in your mind?

How did you feel after viewing or treating another person as an object to be used or abused?

Have you ever allowed yourself to be treated as less than a child of God who was created and redeemed, justified and adopted? How? Why?

Those last three questions may have been especially difficult to respond to or even think about. That's because their root is shame. The human desire to hide and escape from these feelings goes back to the beginning of history. But so does the promise that God will make things right again, recovering innocence and honor.

There's a way out from the heart-numbing cycle of guilt and shame, anger, abuse, and lust.

You're not cheap and worthless. Christ died on the cross in your place. The sovereign King says you're unbelievably valuable.

THIS IS A GOOD TIME TO COME BEFORE THE KING OF GLORY, YOUR LOVING FATHER, AND REPENT. TAKE OWNERSHIP OF YOUR ANGER, ABUSE, AND LUST AND TURN FROM THEM. GOD HAS AN ANSWER. HIS GOSPEL CAN ABSOLUTELY STOP THE MADNESS OF THIS CYCLE. LET HIM IN AND LET HIS SPIRIT WORK ON YOUR HEART.

6.3

THE GOSPEL OF GRACE—BEING FULLY KNOWN

We need peace. The storm feels overwhelming, even as Christ-followers.

Sometimes the answer we need comes in the form of a question.

And as we begin to sort through the wreckage in the wake of our guilt and shame, Jesus' question to His disciples points us to our source of hope and freedom.

READ LUKE 8:22-25.

Put yourself in the boat as one of Jesus' disciples. Remember that some of these guys were fishermen and had surely endured extreme weather conditions. Their reaction indicates that this was an intense storm.

When have you felt that even Jesus didn't care if you were perishing?

What did you do in desperation for relief?

Consider the storms resulting from your guilt and shame—the anger, abuse, and lust that rage in your life. What's your response when Jesus asks, "Where is your faith?"

What reality check does Jesus' rebuke of the wind and waves provide in your life? Are you, like the disciples, in awe of His power? How are you allowing Him to speak into your heart?

The word of God has power. It calms storms. But like the disciples, we have to do a little soul-searching when face-to-face with such sovereign power. We must question what we believe about Jesus and whether we'll trust, obey, and find our identity in Him.

When we find ourselves humbled before Him, the Word of God brings conviction. And remember, all guilt and shame isn't unhealthy. Being trapped and diving deeper into a destructive pattern is unhealthy. Feeling an urgent dependence on Christ is life-giving. We know godly grief leads to repentant faith—surrendering to Him in humility.

So don't dismiss conviction. But let it steer you out of that downward spiral you've been stuck in.

READ JOHN 16:7-8.

What does Jesus promise to give to His followers?

If you've ever felt that life would be easier if Jesus were with you in flesh and blood, what does He say here?

What role does the Spirit of God play in dealing with the guilt of sin?

Nothing drives away shame faster than being fully known and yet still loved, enjoyed, and delighted in by the One who knows you best. Shame begins to vanish when we realize we can be truly vulnerable and confess our sin before God and before others, especially fellow brothers and sisters in Christ. The best way to make sure shame can't take root in your heart—and can't naturally grow into anger, abuse, and lust—is to free yourself from all secrets.

Your Creator knows everything about you. As the perfectly just Judge, He knows every guilty offense—past, present, and future. Yet as your adoptive Father, He delights in you, chasing out any trace of shame. You're free in Him. All His children are free. Share in the joy of that freedom among the community of believers.

Let's look back at a story dealing with a downward spiral, a right response to guilt and shame, and redemptive love.

READ LUKE 15:11-32.

> How does the father in this story deal with his sons' guilt and shame?

Most likely, even if nobody but God knows certain secrets about you, the weight of those secrets is the root beneath almost all your depression, your disgust with yourself, your coolness toward worship, and your obsession with keeping yourself covered and mysterious.

READ 1 JOHN 3:20.

> What guilt and shame are in your heart right now? How will you trust God, whose love is greater than the guilt He already knows about?

> Knowing you're fully known and delighted in by your Father what happens to your shame and the burdensome weight of your secrets?

> How does that awareness help you accept yourself, delight in God, and be open with others?

The gospel gives it all. Justification to set you free from guilt. Adoption to replace your secret shame. Sanctification for deconstructing your false ideals.

READ 1 THESSALONIANS 5:12-24.

What encouragement does this Scripture provide regarding the freedom of being fully known in godly community?

READ PSALM 103.

What do verses 8-12 say about God's love for you and His dealing with your sin?

How does this psalm offer hope for a life free from shame?

Write a psalm of your own, praising God for knowing you fully and for loving you perfectly.

THANK GOD THAT HE HAS CANCELED YOUR RECORD OF DEBT, TAKING AWAY YOUR GUILT. THANK HIM FOR THE SANCTIFYING WORK OF HIS SPIRIT, MAKING YOU HOLY AND HEALING YOU. THANK HIM THAT HE HAS ADOPTED YOU AS HIS CHILD AND DELIGHTS IN YOU. IF YOU NEED TO ACCEPT HIS LOVE FOR YOU, DO THAT NOW AS YOU PRAY.

TRUSTING GOD'S GOODNESS: FREE FROM FEAR

BEGIN YOUR DISCUSSION WITH THE ACTIVITY BELOW.

There was some heavy stuff in session 6. What encouraged you? What challenged you?

In this session we shift our attention from the toxic cycle of shame to the other most common and unhealthy trap we find ourselves in—fear.

On a scale of 0–10 (10 being greatest), how significant have fear and anxiety been in shaping your life?

What kinds of things do you tend to be most anxious about?

What one thing in your life are you most worried about right now?

TO PREPARE FOR THE VIDEO, READ ALOUD FROM ISAIAH 43:1-7:

> *Thus says the LORD,*
> *he who created you, O Jacob,*
> *he who formed you, O Israel:*
> *"Fear not, for I have redeemed you;*
> *I have called you by name, you are mine.*
> *When you pass through the waters, I will be with you;*
> *and through the rivers, they shall not overwhelm you;*
> *when you walk through fire you shall not be burned,*
> *and the flame shall not consume you.*
> *For I am the LORD your God,*
> *the Holy One of Israel, your Savior. ...*
> *You are precious in my eyes,*
> *and honored, and I love you. ...*
> *Fear not, for I am with you ...*
> *everyone who is called by my name,*
> *whom I created for my glory,*
> *whom I formed and made."*

WATCH

COMPLETE THE VIEWER GUIDE BELOW AS YOU WATCH SESSION 7.

We have to do something with fear and anxiety because it is not in line with God's good and right _____ .

The more value you give specific things, the more _____ and _____ will rule and reign around those things.

If you exalt your children too much, your fear over them will _____ you and rob you of the enjoyment of them.

Work hard, be good stewards, and then trust the _____ .

The weapon we have been given to fight fear and anxiety is _____ that God is ultimately good and reigns and rules over our lives in a way that is more rich in wisdom than our own reign over our lives.

It is a freeing thing to understand you have no _____ .

The worst thing you can do with fear and anxiety is pretend you're _____ and don't have it.

You will not use God for bread. You will get God, and He will be _____ .

The bottom line in most fear and anxiety is you simply don't trust that God is _____ .

The Lord's invitation to us, repeatedly, is to walk in the _____ .

Video sessions available for purchase
at *www.lifeway.com/recoveringredemption*

DISCUSS THE VIDEO SEGMENT, USING THE QUESTIONS BELOW.

What did you most need to hear in today's video?

This session continues our practical exploration of sanctification. How do fear and anxiety block us from growing in holiness and becoming more and more like Jesus?

Matt warned us about how much value we attach to certain things. The more value we assign, the more fear and anxiety we'll have in regard to those things. How have you seen that play out in the following areas?

☐ Money/finances

☐ Family/children

☐ Work

☐ Health

☐ Other:

React to Matt's statement: "The bottom line in most fear and anxiety is you simply don't trust that God is good."

Matt said it's no help to pretend you trust God: "Fear and anxiety are never going to lose their power over you until you can be honest about what drives them, namely that you don't trust that God is good." Matt talked about bringing this fear into the light and confessing it before others. This is a safe place for you to do that.

How do you struggle with trusting that God is good—or at least with believing that He will be good to you?

Close by reading aloud Lamentations 3:22-23 before praying for one another. Pray that you'll each have the strength to trust in God's goodness today. Thank God that He already knows about tomorrow. Praise Him for His loving care for you.

READ SESSION 7 AND COMPLETE THE PERSONAL STUDY BEFORE THE NEXT GROUP EXPERIENCE.

CONSIDER GOING DEEPER INTO THIS CONTENT BY READING CHAPTER 8 IN MATT CHANDLER AND MICHAEL SNETZER'S BOOK RECOVERING REDEMPTION *(B&H, 2014).*

TRUSTING GOD'S GOODNESS: FREE FROM FEAR

We can't live in the silver lining forever. Eventually, we get sucked into the dark middle of life's storms.

This is the attitude haunting too many of our minds. This thought pattern, like the downward spiral of guilt and shame, can be an endless burden to carry. It's a paralyzing and crushing weight, robbing each day of its joy and abundance.

Though it's true that life isn't always easy and hardship inevitably comes— we've seen that persevering through various trials is part of how our Father grows us in maturity. God isn't out to get us. Christ didn't redeem us just so that we could then tiptoe through life, waiting for the other shoe to drop.

God has more for His children.

Redemption brings freedom from the cruel slavery of fear, releasing us from the anxiety that cripples our daily walk with Christ.

7.1

PEACE & PROSPERITY

Think back to the garden of Eden. Remember the ideal reality into which God created mankind—the state of perfect relationship that continues to stir a jealous longing inside us, drawing us toward the only One who can remake what's been broken.

Within this paradise at the beginning of time, before the introduction of sin, shame, and chaos, we saw (in session 1) a quality woven through the canvas of creation—*shalom.* That peace and prosperity are a stark contrast to the fear and anxiety characterizing so many lives today.

QUICKLY READ GENESIS 1:27-31; 2:1-15.

> Describe in your own words the presence of peace and prosperity—not meaning riches but satisfaction and provision. Consider Adam and Eve's work, relationships, needs, and pleasure.

QUICKLY READ GENESIS 3:16-19.

> How did fear and anxiety replace the perfect peace and prosperity of God's design?

> How do you experience the unsettled longing inside you for the peace and prosperity of God's original design?

The peace and prosperity that existed in the lives of Adam and Eve before the fall weren't goals they sought for themselves and had somehow been able to attain. Ease and abundance weren't a calculated pursuit of desired circumstances and living conditions. No, the Source of their confidence was simply God alone. As long as they were in fellowship with Him, they could forever expect His blessings to roll into their lives.

He was their righteousness. He was their innocence. He was their dignity and honor. He defined their identity. He was their peace. And He was their prosperity.

Experiencing His goodness left no room for fear or anxiety.

And though mankind chose to veer away from being satisfied in the Creator, God didn't abandon us.

READ LUKE 2:10-14.

> What specific words or phrases jump out at you in the announcement of Jesus' birth?

READ 2 CORINTHIANS 1:3 AND WRITE IT BELOW.

> What hope does this verse provide?

Over and over we see God described as Father. For some people, this is a hang-up. We don't all have great memories—or any memories—of a loving father. Even if we had a godly father, we start to see flaws and shortcomings as we grow older. We all know what a father should be. In fact, that innate knowledge of what a father should be is why any shortcoming is so painful. But our Heavenly Father isn't like earthly fathers.

READ LUKE 11:11-13.

> How is God described?

> What hope do these verses provide?

READ JAMES 1:17 AND WRITE IT BELOW.

What hope does this verse provide?

Your Heavenly Father is good. Nothing changes that. Not even your own stubborn rebellion or timid anxiety. He wasn't just good at the beginning; He's good today.

The world is broken—yes. Relationships are busted up. The created order has fallen into chaos. But He's not caught off guard or pushed around by anything that seems too big for you, no matter what it is. He gives you everything you need and more.

The same Jesus who calms storms with the power of His word (see Luke 8:22-25) can recover peace and prosperity in the hearts of God's children.

READ PSALM 62:5-8.

Describe the psalmist's attitude toward fear or anxiety.

Pause now to write your own prayer of praise:

God alone is my …

CONTINUE IN PRAYER, ADDRESSING GOD AS FATHER AND THANKING HIM FOR HIS PRESENCE WITH YOU AND HIS DESIRE TO BE IN RELATIONSHIP WITH YOU.

7.2

THE OPPOSITE OF WORRY

Peace and prosperity have been choked out by a deep-rooted fear. This produces all kinds of unhealthy patterns of thought and behavior. But just as Christ provided an exit from the downward spiral of guilt and shame, He also brings freedom from fear.

Contrary to what may seem logical, freedom comes from surrendering control—or rather the illusion of control. God is sovereign. We are not.

Everything around us is capable of becoming an idol that drains away our trust in the sufficiency and sovereignty of God. Anything put in God's rightful place—anything we allow to determine our worth, our identity, or our joy—begins to instill fear and anxiety.

It's a cruel irony. But it's always true. Overvaluing anything—even a good and needed thing—spins us into an endless, futile cycle of trying to protect the fragile system of satisfaction we've constructed around that false god.

READ MATTHEW 6:25-34.

Why do you think Jesus talked about worry and anxiety to His disciples?

What do you tend to be anxious about? Check the matters you worry most about.

☐ Money/finances

☐ Family/children

☐ Work

☐ Health

☐ Other:

For the areas you've indicated, write what you worry about and why, how it feels inside, and how that fear expresses itself outwardly.

What do you find to be the most encouraging—and the most needed reminder when tempted to worry—in Matthew 6:25-34? Write it here.

What's the underlying truth in Jesus' illustration of birds and grass?

In our previous session, out in the storm Jesus asked His followers, "Where is your faith?" (Luke 8:25). Now He says, "O you of little faith" (Matt. 6:30). Freedom always comes down to faith. It always comes back to the redemption found only in the gospel.

Faith is the opposite of worry.

Underneath all fear and anxiety is the simple fact that we don't believe—don't have faith—in the goodness of God. To be a worrier means we don't trust He's going to provide for us, we don't think He's looking out for our best interests, or we don't feel convinced that He's wise enough to know what to do for us.

Fear doubts God's goodness.

Using your previous list of ways you're prone to worry, identify how the root of each fear is evidence of not trusting God's goodness. In other words, if you believed God was good and would be good to you, how would that dispel your fear?

There are reasons you don't trust God's goodness. Understandable reasons, in fact.

Perhaps your heart's been seriously betrayed by people in your past, and now you aren't willing to risk vulnerability.

Perhaps you've seen enough things go wrong in life that you're cautious and skeptical, unable to wrap your heart and mind around grace.

Perhaps you don't feel worthy of anything good, still believing that cosmic scales exist and could never tip in your favor.

Or is it a combination of these? Is it something else?

Why don't you trust God? Where does fear stem from in your life? Sit silently with that question in your mind for a minute or two. Then respond as best you can.

Now to be clear, faith doesn't mean an absence of fear. It means facing fear and trusting that God's goodness is greater. Your Father's desire is to walk you straight through your fears to the other side, proving that you didn't really have anything to be afraid of in the first place. Not when you know the Prince of peace (see Isa. 9:6).

The more you trust God, the less anxiety you experience. The grip of fear that was once so tight—choking the life out of you and squeezing the joy from every good gift—loosens until it eventually lets go. Freedom exists in realizing that God is increasingly becoming your primary love, rightfully in the place that so many other things used to occupy in your heart. He's infinitely greater than anything in this broken world.

So how do you break free from fear and anxiety, surrendering control of your life?

READ PHILIPPIANS 4:4-7.

What practical antidotes to anxiety are prescribed in this passage?

God's Spirit is with you and Christ is coming soon. How can remembering that "the Lord is at hand" (v. 5) keep your worries in perspective? How is it the reasonable response to even the most stressful situations?

How can God's peace surpass your understanding?

From what do your heart and mind need to be guarded?

If you're battling the constant attack of anxiety, ask for relief right now. God knows. But making your request known is a step of surrender, releasing that fear into His sovereign hands. Counter those anxious feelings with rejoicing. We'll look more at becoming experts in thankfulness in session 11.

When you're ruled by anxiety, there are few things more frustrating than simply being told not to worry. But Scripture recovers the peace of God by mortifying the old habit of worry, replacing it with a new pattern of rejoicing, prayer, and gratitude for God's goodness. Choose to trust the sovereignty and goodness of your Redeemer.

PRAY NOW, USING PHILIPPIANS 4:4-7 AS YOUR GUIDE. REJOICE, GIVE THANKS, AND LET YOUR REQUESTS BE KNOWN TO THE GOD OF PEACE.

7.3

WIN THE DAY

You have a choice to make. A grace-enabled choice.

Are you going to believe, as Jesus promised, that "each day has enough trouble of its own" (Matt. 6:34, HCSB)?

> Right now what are you tempted to worry about, borrowing stress from tomorrow and robbing yourself of whatever God has for you today?

Take those runaway thoughts captive (remember 2 Cor. 10:5), making them submit to the sovereign grace of your Lord.

Each day may be a struggle—a battle in your mind. But Jesus has secured ultimate victory.

READ JOHN 16:33 AND WRITE IT IN THE SPACE BELOW.

READ 1 JOHN 5:4 AND WRITE IT IN THE SPACE BELOW.

Do you believe that He's given you everything you need—that He's everything you need—to get through today? Not just to survive but to win the day?

GO BACK AND READ MATTHEW 6:19-34.

> In your own words, explain what it means and practically looks like to "store up … treasures in heaven" (v. 20).

Notice *therefore* in verse 25. What relation is there between what you treasure, what you look to as sovereign, and what you worry about?

In your own words, explain what it means and practically looks like for you to "seek first his kingdom and his righteousness" (v. 33).

Remember, you don't have to pretend you're not scared. You actually have to admit your fears. Face them. Let God lead you through them. Be brave enough to say, "I'm afraid of this thing." And don't worry about what people may think about what you worry about. Are you starting to see the insanely circular nature of these traps we get stuck in? They drive us inward, isolating us from the freedom found only in community centered on the gospel. Trust requires relationship.

READ PSALM 56.

Look for words and phrases in which David admitted, "I'm afraid of this thing." How would you characterize David's view of his fear and anxiety?

Now look for verses in which David expressed his understanding of God's goodness and greatness. How did he view God?

How does David's response model healthy freedom in dealing with fear and anxiety?

Being a child of the King means being part of His family. Eventually, we'll have to deal with our dirty laundry. Today would be a good day to get this stuff out into the open and break free from the anxiety-filled delusion that you are in control.

READ JOHN 3:16-21.

What do these verses say about God's desire for you?

For what reasons do people try to keep their lives from being exposed to God's light?

Remember, dealing with our fear and anxiety, dragging these deep roots out into the light, is a practical part of the sanctification process—renewing our minds—putting ourselves into the sovereign hands of God as He conforms us to the image of His Son.

What will you do to bring your fears and anxieties into the light?

READ 1 JOHN 1:5-10.

Pay attention to the words *light* and *darkness* in 1 John 1:5-10, and list below the descriptions and characteristics relating to each.

Light   **Darkness**

What does your list tell you about walking in the light rather than hiding in the darkness?

Your loving Father is calling you into the light. Christ has won victory over sin and death, guilt and shame, fear and anxiety. His Spirit empowers you to step out of the darkness and walk in freedom. Trust Him. God is good.

Take every dissenting thought captive, choosing to focus on today. Let tomorrow worry about itself. God's mercies are new every morning (see Lam. 3:22-23). He's all you need.

Don't live in the darkness of defeat—in fear and anxiety.

Christ saved you. He has more for you.

Win the day.

CLOSE IN PRAYER BY READING PSALM 118:24 AND WRITING IT BELOW. TAKE TIME TO REJOICE AND BE GLAD FOR GOD'S LOVING PROVISION AND PROTECTION.

CONTINUING HEALTHY CYCLES: THE NEW SELF

BEGIN DISCUSSION WITH THE ACTIVITY BELOW.

Fill in the blanks in the sentence below to tell the story of a change in your life.

I was _____, but now I _____.

Examples: I was an art major, but now I work in an accounting firm. I was someone who thought I'd never have kids, but now I have four children.

Today we'll look at how the Christian life is one of continual transformation. We've been changed—instantaneously justified and adopted—but growing to maturity in sanctification is an ongoing process.

What questions or insights do you have from your personal study of session 7?

What new freedom have you experienced as you've studied the cycles of guilt and shame, fear and anxiety?

TO PREPARE FOR THE VIDEO, READ ALOUD 1 PETER 2:9-11:

You are a chosen race, a royal priesthood, a holy nation, a people for his own possession, that you may proclaim the excellencies of him who called you out of darkness into his marvelous light. Once you were not a people, but now you are God's people; once you had not received mercy, but now you have received mercy. Beloved, I urge you as sojourners and exiles to abstain from the passions of the flesh, which wage war against your soul.

WATCH

COMPLETE THE VIEWER GUIDE BELOW AS YOU WATCH SESSION 8.

Every one of us was _____ in our trespasses and sins, and we followed in the way of the _____.

We were by our nature objects of God's _____.

Wrath is God allowing men to pursue the very things they want to pursue that will kill them, all the while patiently waiting for them to realize it's a dead end, and they'll _____ to Him.

Common graces are _____ outside of knowing the Lord.

Even as God's wrath steadily builds toward an individual, there are common graces that are given to that person, hopefully so they might realize there is something _____ that.

We were _____, and dead men have roots that go deep. Those roots are the roots of guilt and shame, of fear and anxiety, and then the _____ of those roots bear in all sorts of different ways.

We have been made _____ with Christ. Those roots are being pulled up.

God so loves you that He will ruthlessly garden in the _____ of your heart.

For you to just have the _____ of sin removed while the _____ remains is no good for you and brings no glory to God.

Throughout the ages you'll see that He's _____, that there's never a moment where there's not more of Him to know, more of Him to be experienced, more joy to be had.

We _____ our former ways while simultaneously _____ in who we are.

Get over yourself. It's _____ who does the good work.

Day by day, being renewed in the inner man, renouncing the old ways, rerooting in the new, we ask and plead with God to strengthen us for the _____ , to give us victory over our sin in the _____ .

Video sessions available for purchase
at *www.lifeway.com/recoveringredemption*

DISCUSS THE VIDEO SEGMENT, USING THE QUESTIONS BELOW.

What did you most need to hear today in Matt's teaching?

Matt talked about living with an ongoing ethic. How have you seen day-to-day discipline to be more effective than an "I want it now" approach?

What does it mean to be alive in Christ Jesus?

How is the Christian life an ongoing ethic?

Matt said when we're feeling guilt, shame, fear, or anxiety, we should take heart because our Heavenly Father lovingly and ruthlessly pulls on the roots of those things in our lives. How does that perspective change the way you look at your guilt and shame, your fear and anxiety?

What does it look like for you to renounce old ways while simultaneously rerooting who you are?

You're God's workmanship, and this is an ongoing project as He builds you up and renews you day by day. What's your part of this process on a daily basis?

Wrap up your time as a group by encouraging people to share specific requests for ways they need God to work in their lives. Take these requests before God and ask for His strength in renouncing and rerooting.

READ SESSION 8 AND COMPLETE THE PERSONAL STUDY BEFORE THE NEXT GROUP EXPERIENCE.

CONSIDER GOING DEEPER INTO THIS CONTENT BY READING CHAPTER 9 IN MATT CHANDLER AND MICHAEL SNETZER'S BOOK RECOVERING REDEMPTION *(B&H, 2014).*

CONTINUING HEALTHY CYCLES: THE NEW SELF

The Christian life is a work in progress. There is no silver bullet. No quick fix. No shortcut. It's a journey.

Yes, you're instantaneously justified and adopted. Yes, your salvation by grace through faith in Jesus changes everything. You belong to God. But growing in holiness—sanctification—is an ongoing process. You've seen all this and have waded through some pretty intense waters to get to this point.

It's time to catch your breath a little bit, regroup, and put together all the pieces you've been given so far. You've explored the depths of unhealthy cycles that suck the joy and freedom out of your Christian life. Now a healthy pattern needs to be put in place.

You're a new creation. But you have to continually take off the old self and put on the new self. This happens with three basic actions:

1. Renouncing what's old

2. Rerooting in what's new

3. Requesting God's help to continue growing

8.1

RENOUNCING WHAT'S OLD

If you're a Christian, your life was deeply rooted in death before God reached down and remade you. You were out of fellowship with your Creator. Whether you were 5 years old or 50, you were grounded in dry soil, in a lifeless grave, disconnected from God. You were held down by and predisposed to a fallen heritage of worldly cravings, guilt and shame, fear and anxiety, selfish ambition and pride, needy cries for approval, and even religious fakery or manipulation.

And some of those roots are tough to pull up.

READ EPHESIANS 2:1-3.

What does it mean to be spiritually dead?

How do these verses reflect what you were before you were saved? Describe your life before Christ.

Being dead in our trespasses and sins and following the course of this world shapes our identities. How we see and understand ourselves affects everything. Let's look back at the four empty wells we first identified in session 1. Each step down these crooked paths was a trespass against our Creator. Take a moment to think about these, and record the way each one demonstrates the futility of being dead in sin.

Seeking a better version of *yourself*:

Thinking *others* will complete you:

Pursuing the things of *the world*:

Engaging in external *religion*:

As we bought into the myth of each of these dry wells, seeking satisfaction down these crooked paths, we revealed ourselves to be enemies of God. Setting ourselves up in opposition to Him, we were objects of God's wrath. It wasn't wrath like the strike of a lightning bolt or the sudden, crashing rush of a tsunami or tidal wave. It was more like a steadily building opposition, an ever-widening distance between God and us.

But His wrath, as we know, is tinged with mercy. In Scripture God's wrath is often seen when He allows people to pursue what they want, knowing it will be their ruin. He patiently draws people from hopeless dead ends so they might cry out for rescue.

When has God allowed you to pursue what you want, knowing it'll be your self-destruction? What was the result?

READ ROMANS 1:18-20; 2:5; 9:22-24.

What do these passages add to your understanding of God's wrath and mercy?

This step in our journey of sanctification involves digging deeper to examine roots of our current struggles with sin. As we've seen, prior to encountering God, we followed the course of the world and attempted to live independently of Him. We developed dysfunctional patterns of sin that ultimately assaulted God's character and His Word.

Idolatry is the ultimate root and source of our sinful patterns—both our former lives in sin and our current struggles with sin. We've worshiped ourselves and other created things rather than the Creator. We're spiritual adulterers.

As we recognize our sinful patterns and their connections to idolatry, we begin the work of renouncing our former ways and offering ourselves to God.

READ JAMES 4:1-10.

What passions and desires still drive you toward sin?

How do you see the concept of idolatry expressed in these verses (see especially vv. 4-5)?

What place does humility need to have as you seek to renounce your old self and your old passions?

What steps have you already taken to renounce who you were, that is, your "friendship with the world" (v. 4)?

CLOSE YOUR TIME IN PRAYER, ASKING GOD TO CONTINUE REVEALING TO YOU AREAS WHERE HE'S CALLING YOU TO RENOUNCE YOUR OLD WAY OF LIFE. REMEMBER, THIS IS SANCTIFICATION, AN ONGOING, DAILY PROCESS! ASK HIM FOR THE HUMILITY NEEDED TO MOVE FORWARD IN RENOUNCING YOUR IDOLATRY. ASK FOR HIS WISDOM AND STRENGTH AS YOU SUBMIT YOURSELF TO HIM TODAY AND AS YOU RESIST THE DEVIL.

REROOTING IN WHAT'S NEW

We're now on a new, forward trajectory from death to life. And though the promise of heaven is as inalterable as His covenant, we know from experience that conversion is only the beginning of the process that uproots these rebellious instincts and attitudes.

Life isn't suddenly perfect, free from conflict with others or even within ourselves. Because deep roots die slowly.

Ephesians 2:1-3 sheds light on the painful reality that our old self was dead. Hopeless.

But God ...

READ EPHESIANS 2:4-9.

How do these verses describe God's character? His attitude toward you?

Describe the gift God has so generously given. What did you do to earn it?

Don't despise the difficult experiences that tug on your heart, making you ache at your core. God knows you'd never be whole if He merely pruned back the bad behavior. Remember, visible fruit is evidence of something deeper inside. God's at work in situations that put pressure on the roots, working to pull up this toxic weed that's destroying you.

Yes, it hurts to feel the roots tearing and splintering. It hurts even more when we're resisting and tugging back from the other end. But there's no other way to keep these roots from flaring back up than for Him to yank on them firmly enough until even the tiniest extremity is up and out of the ground. God loves us too much to let things go so that they can continue to hurt us, continue to hurt others, and continue to keep us from glorifying Him.

So as He unearths those deepest roots—the ones you thought would surely be gone by now—we firmly replant in the healthy, life-giving presence of God. Then new and sanctified roots can grow deep in Him, producing truly satisfying fruit.

Just as mortification requires vivification, renouncing requires rerooting.

With that in mind, fill in the blanks below and then write down anything else that comes to your mind:

I was _____.

But I now renounce that old life because I'm now _____

_____, and I'm rerooting my identity in that.

How have you personally dealt with a recurring problem from a root that just wouldn't die?

In what ways can you see God lovingly working in you, refusing to allow that root to continue draining your spiritual vitality?

READ EPHESIANS 2:10.

Take a moment to soak up the full significance of this Scripture. You're God's workmanship, His masterpiece, His poetry, handcrafted for His purpose. How does this view of being a death-to-life work of God make you feel? What effect does it have on how you see your identity?

How are the good works God has for you a part of this rerooting of yourself into your new way of life?

READ EPHESIANS 4:17-24.

What additional understanding of taking off the old self (renouncing) and putting on the new self (rerooting) does this passage give you?

We were dead in our trespasses and sins. We were following the course and pattern of this world. We were by our very nature an object of God's wrath.

But God made us alive with Him.

And that means it's always the right season to reroot.

No more flirting with forbidden fruit. Instead, we become "Oaks of righteousness, the planting of the LORD, that he may be glorified" (Isa. 61:3).

THANK GOD, YOUR WISE AND STRONG GARDENER, FOR LOVING YOU SO MUCH THAT HE WORKS IN YOUR LIFE TO PULL UP THOSE OLD ROOTS AND TILL THE GROUND OF YOUR HEART TO PLANT YOU IN A NEW WAY OF LIVING. THANK JESUS FOR HIS SACRIFICE OF LOVE TO GIVE YOU NEW, ABUNDANT LIFE. ALLOW YOUR THANKSGIVING TO FLOW INTO PRAISE FOR GOD.

8.3

REQUESTING GOD'S CONTINUAL HELP

READ JOHN 15:1-7.

What did Jesus teach about renouncing, rerooting, and requesting?

What did Jesus teach about the ongoing work of the Vinedresser?

This is imperative. It's your Father who does the good work. He's prepared it for you (see Eph. 2:10). You don't have to be an expert. Just trust and believe that God's going to use you. Find your life in Christ. Dwell in Him and let Him dwell in you. You're a new creation. The old has passed away. The new has come.

Without Him there's no life—you can't produce anything of worth. There's no fruit, and your life is wasted.

In Him there's life—joyful obedience, producing fruit that pleases and glorifies the Father and Son.

Isn't this what you want—new life rooted in Him?

Then ask.

READ 2 CORINTHIANS 4:16-18.

The fact that Paul includes an encouragement not to lose heart tells us that we're not alone when feeling worn out. In the midst of renouncing and rerooting, when are you tempted to grow frustrated or discouraged?

Paul wrote that we're "being renewed day by day" (v. 16). What does that reality indicate about the nature of the process? What does it also reveal about where you are in the process? (Also see Luke 9:23; 11:3.)

The fact that sanctification is a daily process keeps us asking God for strength. We need Him daily. This dependence keeps us from running back down crooked paths, forgetting that every blessing of the gospel is the result of being hidden in Christ.

READ COLOSSIANS 3:1-11.

Think about what it means for you each day to be "hidden with Christ in God" (v. 3) and for Christ to be your life—to be "all" (v. 11). List ways you can live in each of those realities.

I'm Hidden with Christ in God   **Christ Is My Life**

So the asking becomes a daily, ongoing experience as well—of admitting need and being with Him. Of repenting and receiving, of confessing and changing. We don't get bogged down in last year's struggles or worry about tomorrow's trials. We just focus on winning the day. That's the objective: win the day. And we keep walking through the process of renouncing and rerooting day after day, thanking the Vinedresser for not leaving a stone unturned that might block us from enjoying all of Him.

Prayerfully consider and complete the following questions.

God, will You save me today from _____?

Will You help me today with _____?

Will You strengthen me today for _____?

Will You give me discipline today to _____?

Will You give me hope today in the midst of _____?

Will You help me repent today of _____?

Will You embolden me today to confess _____?

Will You give me victory today over _____?

*LOOK AGAIN AT 2 CORINTHIANS 4:16-18. THEN ALSO
READ ROMANS 8:18 AND 1 JOHN 2:17.*

How do these Scriptures encourage you to depend on God?

In what ways are the "things that are unseen" more real than "the things
that are seen" (2 Cor. 4:18)?

What will you do today to keep your eyes on what's eternal?

Ask. Jesus says to ask—constantly. Why wouldn't you? After being brought to life from
death, are you too proud to ask Him for help each day? Your Father knows growing to
maturity isn't an overnight deal; it's a lifelong process.

Renounce. Reroot. Request.

Then do it again tomorrow.

*AS YOU BEGIN TO PRAY, LOOK BACK OVER YOUR LIST OF
QUESTIONS TO TAKE TO GOD TODAY. USE THESE TO GUIDE
YOU AS YOU COMMUNE WITH YOUR HEAVENLY FATHER.*

EXPERIENCING GRACE: LOVE & CONFESSION

SHARE WHAT GOD IS DOING. #RECOVERINGREDEMPTION

BEGIN DISCUSSION WITH THE ACTIVITY BELOW.

> How did your personal time during session 8 go? What did you learn about renouncing, rerooting, and requesting?

> Did you specifically ask for anything?

> What prevents you from continually asking for God's help?

Today our attention takes another turn in this ongoing process of sanctification. We've focused a lot on personal identity and relationship with God. Now we're shifting our attention toward biblical peacemaking—how to reconcile and make amends when our sin affects others around us.

> So let's start with a little poll: How many of you have had a conflict with someone during the past year?

Even though we've been made right in our vertical relationship with God, we still experience drama in our horizontal relationships. Because we've been redeemed by grace, humility and love should characterize all our relationships.

TO PREPARE FOR THE VIDEO, READ ALOUD PSALM 51:1-4:

> *Have mercy on me, O God,*
> *   according to your steadfast love;*
> *according to your abundant mercy*
> *   blot out my transgressions.*
> *Wash me thoroughly from my iniquity,*
> *and cleanse me from my sin!*
> *For I know my transgressions,*
> *and my sin is ever before me.*
> *Against you, you only, have I sinned*
> *and done what is evil in your sight,*
> *so that you may be justified in your words*
> *and blameless in your judgment.*

WATCH

God has righted the vertical relationship, yet I still have issues _____.

We are motivated in how we live our lives by the _____ of God made manifest for us in _____.

We have a tendency to _____ people quickly, to be disappointed quickly, to grow frustrated quickly, and to wound others quickly.

God puts a good weight on His people to work toward _____ whenever we have sinned against others or harmed others, whether we know we did or not.

God has already given us the example of what He would have done: _____ and _____, engage and reconcile.

When you sin against God, there is a ripple effect that creates _____ in the relationships around you.

We must look inside our hearts, see where we have _____ against others, and then seek reconciliation and make amends.

THE ART OF CONFESSION

1. Address _____ involved.

2. Avoid _____, but, and maybe.

3. Admit _____.

4. Acknowledge the _____.

5. Accept the _____.

6. Alter your _____.

7. Ask for _____.

Own your _____.

Video sessions available for purchase
at *www.lifeway.com/recoveringredemption*

DISCUSS THE VIDEO SEGMENT, USING THE QUESTIONS BELOW.

What was most valuable to you in this session?

Matt said, "Despite the fact I have been vertically reconciled to God, even now, horizontally, I still am almost habitually seeking the forgiveness of others." How have you seen that, even during the past week, in your life?

Matt shared seven principles for confession and seeking reconciliation with others (from Ken Sande's "The Seven *A*'s of Confession").[1] Which of these do you find the most difficult to carry out, and why?

1. Address everyone involved (all those you affected).

2. Avoid *if, but,* and *maybe* (don't try to excuse your wrongs).

3. Admit specifically (both attitudes and actions).

4. Acknowledge the hurt (express sorrow for hurting someone).

5. Accept the consequences (such as making restitution).

6. Alter your behavior (change your attitudes and actions).

7. Ask for forgiveness.

Jesus said, "By this all people will know that you are my disciples, if you have love for one another" (John 13:35). At another time He said, "Be at peace with one another" (Mark 9:50). When have you experienced success in peacemaking, using the *A*'s of confession?

What will you do this week to seek reconciliation?

Close in prayer, thanking God for His unwarranted forgiveness. Encourage group members to be motivated by His grace to own their sin and to seek to make peace with others this week.

READ SESSION 9 AND COMPLETE THE PERSONAL STUDY BEFORE THE NEXT GROUP EXPERIENCE.

CONSIDER GOING DEEPER INTO THIS CONTENT BY READING CHAPTER 10 IN MATT CHANDLER AND MICHAEL SNETZER'S BOOK RECOVERING REDEMPTION *(B&H, 2014).*

EXPERIENCING GRACE: LOVE & CONFESSION

Let's be honest. God has righted the vertical relationship, yet we all still have issues horizontally.

Any trouble we may experience in loving others indicates that something isn't squared up in our loving relationship with God. We've received grace, and we are expected to share it freely, extending the love of Christ to those around us.

If reconciliation with other people is ever going to be genuine, not meant to prove a point but simply to demonstrate the love of Christ and the transformation He's brought about in our hearts, then we must first be vertically aligned and at rest in Him. We must know how completely loved we are, and we must overflow with loving gratitude for the grace and forgiveness He's given us through salvation.

Being reconciled to God doesn't suddenly make us immune from sinning against others or from being sinned against by others. But the recovery of redemption does mean that even the way we deal with these horizontal difficulties of life has been thoroughly transformed by the gospel.

After all, if we're following Christ, it'll be evident in our love for one another.

So when we sin against someone—or when we're sinned against—how do we respond with the love of Christ?

9.1

KNOWN BY OUR LOVE

By nature we were separated from our Creator God. In that separation, because of sin, we found ourselves on some crooked paths, trying to satisfy our souls with the empty promises of dry wells.

When we find ourselves on one of those crooked paths, our relationships with others will always suffer collateral damage.

> Reflect back on the four empty wells. Identify specific examples of how the paths leading to each one have also led you into conflict with other people. Use the questions to help you think through each issue.
>
> *Self:* Seeking a better version of yourself. Is life all about you? Are people commodities to you? Are you using others as leverage to get where you want to go? How is this pursuit affecting your relationships?

> *Others:* Looking for other people to complete you. Do you need your spouse, children, friends, or small group to cheer you on and put you uppermost in their affections? Do you have unrealistic expectations of them? Have they become a god to you? How is this pursuit affecting those relationships?

> *The world:* Pursuing the things of the world. Have things of the world become a god to you? Are you using people to gain more of the world? Do other people get in your way or get neglected as you chase more earthly pleasures or possessions? How does that pursuit affect the depth of your relationships?

Religion: Engaging in external religion. Have you developed a rule-based mentality that has no grace for others? Must people measure up to your standards—not God's? Do you compete with or compare your knowledge or righteousness with that of other people? How is this pursuit affecting your relationships?

We know life is messy. In a world filled with broken people, there are going to be collisions. We're going to get hurt. We're going to hurt others. So what do we do?

READ JOHN 13:35.

Think about a difficult relationship in your life. Have you shown that person the gracious love of Christ? How could the average person see the gospel by looking at your attitude toward that relationship?

What does it mean to love someone you've sinned against? What about someone who's sinned against you?

Despite the fact that we're the recipients of an unmeasured amount of grace, we don't tend to give others the benefit of the doubt. We don't tend to be gracious. We have a tendency to attack quickly, to be disappointed quickly, to grow frustrated quickly, and—God help us—to wound others quickly when we feel there's been injustice.

The same glorious realities that sealed our own conversion to Christ should spill over into our daily interactions with others. Our horizontal relationships reflect our vertical relationship—or at least our view of it. If we aren't listening to others, aren't caring about them, aren't valuing them, aren't working for their good, then we have a skewed perspective that doesn't recognize the humbling reality of our own need for ongoing grace and forgiveness. Any fracture in our vertical relationship with God will have a ripple effect horizontally across our daily interaction with other people—other people who are equally in need of redemption—people who are no more or less deserving of the love of Christ than we are.

But in times like these, God will faithfully lean on us with the healthy weight of His grace. He compels us toward necessary action, as a father's strong hand gently guides a child to step forward and own up for what's been done.

Now let's not pretend that it's easy to love others. But let's also not pretend that we're perfectly lovable ourselves. Love isn't easy. It's an act of the will.

READ 1 JOHN 4:7-21.

> What connection exists between God's love for you and your love for others?

> How is God's love perfected, or made complete, in our love for others?

Remember when we looked at renouncing, rerooting, and requesting in the previous session? To better understand what it means for God's love to be perfected in us, let's take a look at what comes after we root ourselves in Christ (abiding) and ask the Father for whatever we need to grow in sanctification (bearing fruit).

READ JOHN 15:8-17.

> What does verse 11 explicitly reveal to be the motivation behind Jesus' teaching on sanctification and the commandment to love?

> Jesus taught His disciples that they should "love one another as I have loved you" (v.12). Describe ways Christ has loved you.

God doesn't just expect us to love one another. He loved us first. He showed us how and enables us to do so. He pursued us in making peace and desires that we respond by pursuing peace with others.

READ 2 CORINTHIANS 5:14-21.

When you think about the way Christ sacrificially loves you, how does that love motivate you to love and seek reconciliation with others?

Think of a person with whom you have a close although strained relationship. When you view this person according to the flesh (see v. 16)—by outward appearances—what could you be missing?

Now think about this person from a viewpoint that's beyond just a human understanding. Think of this person as someone Jesus loves and died for. Try to see this person as Christ sees him or her. What changes when you look at them from this point of view?

How does verse 15 free you from any personal hesitation in extending love, grace, and forgiveness toward another person?

Look at the progression in verses 18–20: (1) Christ reconciled you with Himself, (2) He gave you this ministry of reconciliation, and (3) you're now His ambassador. In what ways is your "ministry of reconciliation" (v. 18) part of God's overall plan?

If we properly understand and want to be shaped by the redemptive power of the gospel, we'll approach this process from an entirely different perspective. Rather than becoming an expert in other people's sins while staying ignorant of our own, we'll take our offenses seriously and concern ourselves with magnifying God's character through our lives. Once again we surrender the illusion of control and trust God with the outcome of our lives.

To conclude, look back over some Scriptures you've studied in previous sessions, laying the foundational truths in your vertical relationship. Record how each one motivates you to pursue peace in your horizontal relationships—for the glory of God and for the good of others. Think in terms of specific relationships, such as with your spouse, children, parents, siblings, church, small group, coworkers, or others.

Romans 5:1-11

Philippians 2:1-16

1 Thessalonians 5:12-24

AS YOU ENTER A TIME OF PRAYER, THINK AGAIN ABOUT HOW YOU TEND TO TREAT PEOPLE IN YOUR LIFE WITH WHOM YOU HAVE DISAGREEMENTS OR OTHER STRUGGLES. PRAY NOW FOR THIS PERSON OR PEOPLE. EVEN IF YOU DON'T KNOW SPECIFIC NEEDS, LIFT THIS PERSON UP TO GOD. THEN ASK GOD TO HELP YOU SEEK RECONCILIATION.

OWNING OUR PART

There's nothing that makes people downshift into fourth-grade-playground behavior like owning up to personal responsibility for conflict. It becomes a goofy game of blaming the other person. Everyone thinks the other person is at fault; you'll notice that nobody seems to see the drama from exactly the same perspective.

Not to make light of any scenario, but there's a common belief that when you're only 10 percent to blame for a conflict, you don't have to own up to it. Instead, you blame the other person, who's 90 percent to blame, for the entire situation.

No, you've still sinned. You've sinned against God and against them. "Well, that sin was only a response to their sin," you might add. It's still sin.

True, the breakdown of blame is rarely 50-50. It typically weighs more heavily on one side or another, but conflict is never completely one-sided. Remember that conflict by definition requires opposing forces; at least two sides have to be involved. One person may have done considerably less to start the fire. They may have handled themselves very patiently and honorably, considering the drama. But they contributed something to the equation. Any part in sin, even when dwarfed by somebody else's majority share, is still sin.

And do we really want to keep score?

READ MATTHEW 7:1-5.

What does Jesus teach about judgment and trying to justify ourselves by keeping score or assigning blame to others?

Hold your finger as close to your eye as possible while reading the next sentence. Notice that your focus shifts to see past it, making it almost invisible. Now hold it against the page, covering those words with it, noting its apparent change in size and your inability to see around it. We often don't see the log in our own eye; the problem is too close.

In what ways can your perspective about your own faults and the faults of others be out of focus from reality?

What attitudes make people obsess over the obscure flaws in others while being blind to their own flaws?

Think of a conflict you've had in which you thought, at least at the time, that the other person was totally at fault; you took no blame in the matter. Now get introspective and ask God to reveal to you what part you played—regardless of how big or small—in the conflict. Write what you need to take responsibility for.

We're actually sinning against God when logs and specks become wedged between the relationships He's provided. Splinters of pride and self-protection distance us from people loved by God—people who need to see His love through us and even people who may be used to reveal more of His love to us, much to our surprise.

God redeemed us, giving us the message of reconciliation as ambassadors of Christ (see 2 Cor. 5:18-21). All unrighteousness in the life of a Christ-follower disregards this God-given identity and fractures the purpose of relationship.

The cross of Christ inextricably binds our vertical and horizontal relationships together. When one side is out of line, we feel strain on the other. The redemptive love of Jesus compels us to be reconciled to the Father and to our brothers and sisters in Christ.

READ NUMBERS 5:5-7.

How is all sin first and foremost against God even when manifested in actions against another person? (For a deeper study on this issue, see Gen. 20:6; 39:9; 2 Sam. 12:13; Ps. 51:4; and 1 Cor. 8:12.)

Think about someone you've wronged. In what specific ways can you make restitution to that person? Financial? Relational? Other ways of making things right?

What does going over and above what you owe the person say about the seriousness of your desire to make things right?

What does it say about how much you value peace and reconciliation in your relationship?

What does it say about the worth of the person you've offended?

Our reconciliation with God begins a new rhythm in our heart—a joyful celebration of His grace and mercy. It compels us to action, humbly leading us back to the dividing lines that separated friends and families, points of tension where we've let others down and broken their hearts, where we haven't embodied the loving grace of Jesus. The Spirit is moving in and through us as the rhythm of reconciliation becomes one fluid motion of vertical worship and a quest for horizontal unity.

READ ROMANS 12:16-18.

What comes to mind when you see the word *harmony?* How does harmony illustrate the way God wants us to live with one another (see v.16)?

"If possible, as far as it depends on you ..." (v.18). What does this phrase reveal about what you should expect from the person you're seeking to reconcile with?

But what about when it isn't possible to make amends? What if the other person won't forgive what I've humbly and genuinely owned in my part of the conflict? And how long do I continue to forgive someone for the specks in their eye while I'm working on the log in my own eye? These questions are nothing new for a Christ-follower. Look at Jesus' conversation with the apostle Peter.

READ MATTHEW 18:21-35.

> How do Jesus' parable and teaching challenge your perspective on perseverance and peacemaking?

READ MATTHEW 5:38-45.

> Contrary to worldly wisdom, what does Jesus teach about absorbing and overlooking the offenses of others? If we're to be known by our love—for the good of others and for the glory of God—then what do you need to do today to go the extra mile in seeking peace in difficult, even unfair, relationships? How will you absorb and overlook offenses against you?

Whenever you're involved in conflict with other people, God remains the Authority—not you. He's in charge of orchestrating what needs to happen next for His purposes. Therefore, what He wants to accomplish in bringing you back into good terms with the people you've harmed or injured is of supreme importance compared to your own desire to justify yourself. The desire is to point to Him, not to ourselves.

GO TO THE LORD IN PRAYER, ASKING FOR HIS HELP, HIS WISDOM, AND HIS STRENGTH AS YOU PURSUE RECONCILIATION WITH OTHERS. BEFORE YOU GO TO MAKE RESTITUTION WITH SOMEONE, CONFESS THE SIN TO GOD. THANK HIM FOR RECONCILING YOU TO HIMSELF THROUGH CHRIST'S SACRIFICE.

THE ART OF CONFESSION

Followers of Jesus are especially affected by and dependent on relationships with one another. Our adoption as children of God automatically grafts us into the network of horizontal connections known as the body of Christ, the church (see John 15).

Yet these relationships—even those within the church and small groups—often deteriorate, leading to conflict, strife, and division. As people forgiven by God, we can humbly approach those who've been affected by our sin and make amends. We can apologize, seek reconciliation, and work to reverse the damage we've caused. This change of heart brings glory to God and demonstrates His power by reconciling people to Himself.

READ MATTHEW 5:9.

According to Jesus, who are children of God? What are the implications of this identification and promise?

In what ways have you been blessed by being a peacemaker?

READ GALATIANS 6:7.

How does this principle of reaping and sowing apply to peacemaking?

After examining your own heart, dealing with any logs that distort your perspective, and seeking godly wisdom, you seek reconciliation. Always be sure you are entering confession with a heart that's fully repentant, accepted, and forgiven by God, with your only aim being to establish peace, if peace indeed can be won.

Now, this is critical: make no excuses. No *ifs, buts,* or *maybes*. Using *if, but,* or *maybe* isn't a confession. It's an accusation.

No trying to build platforms for your sins on the basis of the other person's words or actions. No minimizing your part—no matter how small a percentage. Own your part fully and without exception or reservation.

Who comes to mind when considering someone your sin has affected? Using Ken Sande's "Seven *A*'s of Confession," prayerfully identify specific action steps, creating a script of sorts to use as you seek peace.

Address everyone involved (all those whom you affected).

Avoid *if, but,* and *maybe* (don't try to excuse your wrongs).

Admit specifically (both attitudes and actions).

Acknowledge the hurt (express sorrow for hurting someone).

Accept the consequences (such as making restitution).

Alter your behavior (change your attitudes and actions).

Ask for forgiveness.

You have no control over how they respond to your confession.

Your part is to specifically name what you've done, acknowledge pain and difficulty you've added to their life, and then leave the ball in their court. Realize they can take the amount of time necessary to accept your apology and hopefully rebuild what you've contributed in breaking.

But even your most humble, genuine expression of repentance and confession will be susceptible to being shrugged off, rebuffed, or angrily thrown back in your face. Remember, there are no silver bullets.

And you have to be OK with that. Sometimes the minimum goal of peacemaking must be accepted—at least temporarily—as the maximum payoff. You can't demand reciprocity or guarantee a hug and handshake at the end.

READ ROMANS 12:18 (AGAIN—THIS CAN'T BE OVEREMPHASIZED).

"If possible," and "so far as it depends on you" acknowledge the reality that reciprocity won't always exist when seeking to "live peaceably with all." How will you prepare yourself for the potential of needing to absorb and overlook an offense, having done everything within your power to make peace? Write a reminder to yourself in the space below to own your part and to move on if needed.

READ 1 PETER 3:13-17.

How does this passage apply to seeking peace?

As you go to someone seeking peace, forgiveness, and reconciliation, how can the command to "in your hearts honor Christ the Lord as holy" (v. 15) help you?

How might seeking peace be a witness or testimony to the person from whom you're seeking it or to someone else?

How can suffering for doing good affect your conscience?

IN PRAYER ASK GOD TO FORGIVE YOU FOR NOT DOING YOUR PART TO RECONCILE THESE BROKEN RELATIONSHIPS. ASK HIM TO GRANT YOU THE COURAGE TO SEEK OUT AND MAKE PEACE WITH THOSE YOU'VE SINNED AGAINST. ASK HIM FOR THE ABILITY TO SURRENDER ANY EXPECTATIONS FOR THE OTHER PERSON'S RESPONSE TO YOUR ATTEMPTS TO MAKE AMENDS. LEAVE THE RESULTS TO HIM.

1. Ken Sande, *The Peacemaker: A Biblical Guide to Resolving Conflict* (Grand Rapids: Baker Books, 1997), 126.

MAKING PEACE: CONFRONTING SIN

BEGIN DISCUSSION WITH THE ACTIVITY BELOW.

> What specific questions or insights did you come away with from your personal study of session 9?

> We were encouraged to seek reconciliation with someone we've sinned against—owning our part in the conflict fully and without excuse. What steps have you taken so far?

> Which do you find more difficult: asking someone for forgiveness when you've sinned against them, forgiving someone who confesses they've sinned against you, or confronting someone who's sinned against you? Why?

Conflict, as we know, is always two-sided. In any conflict we first need to examine the log in our own eyes, owning our part in sinning against others. Only then, Jesus says, can we clearly see and genuinely seek what's helpful to others. In this session we'll discuss how (and how not) to deal with a conflict when someone sins against you.

TO PREPARE FOR THE VIDEO, READ ALOUD 1 CORINTHIANS 13:4-7:

> *Love is patient and kind; love does not envy or boast; it is not arrogant or rude. It does not insist on its own way; it is not irritable or resentful; it does not rejoice in wrongdoing, but rejoices with the truth. Love bears all things, believes all things, hopes all things, endures all things.*

WATCH

COMPLETE THE VIEWER GUIDE BELOW AS YOU WATCH SESSION 10.

WAYS WE AVOID CONFLICT

1. We _____.

The first and primary way a Christian deals with being sinned against is by _____ or overlooking the offense.

When the offense can no longer be absorbed or overlooked, a root of _____ is growing in your heart.

2. We _____ away.

You will not find the workplace, neighborhood, or church where you will not be disappointed and _____ against.

Aggressors like to _____, bully, and badger with Scripture.

Part of Christian maturation is to be _____ in our sinfulness by those we have sinned against or those who have noticed our sinfulness.

Speaking the truth in love says, "I am not willing for you to be harmed in ways that have _____ ramifications."

Love is willing to risk the relationship for the good of the _____ of the one being confronted.

They are revealing with their action that they do not possess belief, so our interaction with them becomes the removal of membership and interacting with them as though they're _____.

If there has never been any transformation in your life, and you have no concern about Christ, no desire to follow Him, and no willingness to walk in obedience, you're not a _____.

Bitterness is uprooted when we take steps toward _____.

The more we're willing to _____ one another in a dynamic way, _____ our sin, and _____ one another in a way that says, "I love you enough to risk this," the more robust, deep, and beautiful this community of faith will become.

Video sessions available for purchase
at *www.lifeway.com/recoveringredemption*

DISCUSS THE VIDEO SEGMENT, USING THE QUESTIONS BELOW.

What questions or insights do you have from Matt's teaching?

Matt presented two nonbiblical (but natural) responses to conflict—avoidance and aggression. Which do you naturally gravitate toward?

1. Avoidance responses: Are you more likely to deny the conflict exists, take flight, and remove yourself from the situation or to go passive-aggressive, taking jabs at the person?

2. Aggressive responses: Do you intimidate, bully, badger with Scripture, slander, gossip, or hurt the person (even under a misguided sense of justice)?

What consequences have you witnessed from handling conflict poorly?

What peace have you experienced when handling conflict biblically—the truth was spoken in love, the goal was to win a brother or a sister, and the person was restored? Without sharing any names or anything confidential, what encouragement can you share?

In what environment do you find it most difficult to deal with conflict in a biblical manner, and why?

Speaking the truth in love should come easier for us when we're in a healthy community in which we can trust one another, take off our masks, and share life, for better and worse. How have you experienced this freedom, hopefully among this group?

Conclude in prayer, asking for bold humility and genuine motives in biblical peace-making. Thank God for His grace in Jesus Christ. Pray that He will be glorified as we show love to win brothers and sisters to the Father.

READ SESSION 10 AND COMPLETE THE PERSONAL STUDY BEFORE THE NEXT GROUP EXPERIENCE.

CONSIDER GOING DEEPER INTO THIS CONTENT BY READING CHAPTER 11 IN MATT CHANDLER AND MICHAEL SNETZER'S BOOK RECOVERING REDEMPTION (B&H, 2014).

MAKING PEACE: CONFRONTING SIN

Now that we have the log out of our own eye, we can clearly see to help our brothers and sisters.

Like sanctification, peacemaking is an inside-out process that doesn't happen in isolation. We always have to begin with introspection, allowing God to bring desired change in ourselves. Then, from love and a desire to glorify the Father, we humbly extend the redemptive power of Christ to bring freedom and healing to others.

We confront others in their sin not to build an airtight case against them or to exert superior, spiritual control over them but to exhort them toward joy and harmony in their faith.

It's not comfortable. But it's not about us. It's necessary for their sake. It could make an eternal difference in their lives and in the lives of others—literally.

We have nothing more to gain from these conversations than the restoration of our brother or sister.

That's the only win we're after.

10.1

WRONG RESPONSES: FLIGHT OR FIGHT

You will be sinned against.

Nobody needed to tell you that. But what you do need to be constantly reminded of is how to respond in love and grace as a child of God, because it doesn't come naturally.

READ JAMES 3:13-18.

> Contrast the characteristics of relationships handled in worldly wisdom with those led by godly wisdom. What fruit does each harvest?

Worldly Wisdom   **Godly Wisdom**

A word of caution: confronting sin can go horribly wrong. So it's important to be aware of two wrong responses that come naturally when facing conflict—avoidance and aggression. The natural, earthly, worldly way of responding to conflict is flight or fight.

So what does avoidance look like, specifically? The first way we avoid conflict is denial. We just want to deny that we've actually been sinned against.

> When you're faced with conflict, especially when someone has wronged you, do you avoid that person, situation, or topic? What examples of avoiding conflict through denial can you identify in your life?

> How can you tell when healthy deflection (absorbing or overlooking the offense) has crossed the line into unhealthy denial?

Instead of living in trustful dependence on God and with a desire for gospel-based peace and unity with others, we easily slip into a pattern of behavior driven by fear, pride, anger, and a noticeable tolerance for division.

One warning sign for crossing this line from healthy to unhealthy is when we begin to detect in our hearts what the Bible calls a "root of bitterness" (Heb. 12:15). This is a refusal to let something go. The cruel irony is that the poison from a root of bitterness hurts us as much as or more than the person we're refusing to confront and forgive.

READ HEBREWS 12:14-15.

> Think about the things that can cause bitterness, like disappointment, which then lead to resentment and holding grudges. Evaluate your heart. What bitterness is rooted in your heart that may keep you from a healthy, helpful relationship with someone who's sinned against you?

> What will you do with this root of bitterness? Ask the Holy Spirit to remove it from your heart so that you can move forward in seeking peace. Write down any additional thoughts you have.

A second indicator of unhealthy conflict avoidance is when your knee-jerk reaction is to run away from the problem, to simply remove yourself from uncomfortable or upsetting situations in which you're being hurt. As proof of how ineffective this denial tactic is, notice how often it becomes a repeated pattern, a reflex. If this is your tendency, before long you'll run from one church to another, from one group of friends to another, from one source of disharmony to another until you've run through all your relationships and still haven't found a resting place of peace.

If drama seems to follow you everywhere you go, it's for two reasons. First, as you've seen by now, you're the problem. Your own sin keeps you in the middle of conflict. You're running with a log in your eye down crooked paths toward things that can never satisfy your soul (*self*, *others*, *the world*, *religion*). Second, if you're constantly avoiding the hard work of peacemaking, you're leaving a trail of conflict behind you. You keep tripping over the same problems because you never want to help clean up the messes you've helped make.

READ PROVERBS 27:17.

Picture a blade being fashioned on an anvil. Do your relationships endure the hard work of improving one another—hammering out the rough spots—or do you see sparks flying and fear you can't handle the pressure involved in forging a stronger relationship?

Review your past history. When have you tended to run away from conflict? Think about work situations in which you quit a job rather than deal with a tough boss or coworker. Or consider relationships. Have you literally "unfriended" someone to avoid having to deal with conflict? How many small groups have you been in? How many churches have you gone to? Have you left any of these to avoid dealing with conflict?

On the other end of the spectrum from avoidance responses, of course, are aggressive responses—taking matters into our own hands.

This is the "Vengeance is mine" response to sin. (But it is us speaking, not the Lord.)

READ ROMANS 12:19.

How does our aggressive response toward sin against us demonstrate a distrust of God's justice (much as anxiety revealed a distrust of God's goodness)?

If you're in Christ, your identity has been redeemed, but what tendencies do you see in your own relationships to use words, influence, or even Scripture to attack others or highlight something undesirable in them, making yourself look better in contrast?

Honestly, how do you feel justified in wanting others to pay or suffer for ways they've hurt you?

How are you exalting yourself rather than your risen Redeemer, Christ?

What causes an aggressive response in you? When, where, or around whom are you most prone to fight?

Which extreme do you lean toward? Plot your natural responses to conflict. If you're sometimes an avoider and other times an aggressor, write specific names along the continuum to indicate your tendency in that relationship.

1	2	3	4	5	6	7	8	9	10
AVOIDANCE									AGGRESSION

IN PRAYER ADMIT TO GOD YOUR UNHEALTHY, UNBIBLICAL WAYS OF RESPONDING TO CONFLICT, ESPECIALLY WHEN OTHERS HAVE SINNED AGAINST YOU. ASK HIM TO REMOVE ANY BITTERNESS YOU HAVE THAT CAUSES YOU TO AVOID THE ISSUES AND THE PEOPLE INVOLVED. ASK FOR HIS STRENGTH TO STAND FIRM WHEN SOMETHING INSIDE YOU CALLS YOU TO RUN FROM CONFLICT. ASK GOD TO HELP YOU TRUST HIM RATHER THAN SEEKING REVENGE ON YOUR OWN TERMS. WHATEVER IT IS, SURRENDER IT TO HIM.

10.2

RIGHT RESPONSES: ABSORB OR SPEAK THE TRUTH

Proverbs are wise sayings that reveal general principles for godly living. They aren't all intended to offer formulaic truth; sinful people in a broken world aren't entirely predictable. But as rules of thumb for owning our share of the responsibility in life, proverbs point us in the right direction, encouraging us to grow in spiritual maturity.

READ PROVERBS 12:16; 15:1; 19:11; 29:11.

What do these passages teach you about handling conflict wisely?

How have you found that absorbing or overlooking the conflict and having a gentle response work in dealing with conflict?

Name specific instances in which it would be best for you to move past the way you were offended, humbly recognizing the person's spiritual immaturity (or lack of any spiritual life in Christ).

Sometimes sin can't and shouldn't be absorbed or overlooked. There are times when it needs to be dealt with for the sanctification of those involved.

READ EPHESIANS 4:15-16.

Look at the context of these verses. What are the purpose and goal for speaking the truth in love?

Don't use this verse to thinly disguise aggressive words.

When we bring a concern to a brother or sister's attention or when they courageously point out to us a matter of sin in our own lives, the objective must not be fault-finding but rather a desire to help each other mature in relationship with Jesus.

This is how God in His mercy deals with our sin. Not to shame us. Not to manipulate us. No carrot sticks or litmus tests for earning His reluctant approval. But in love. For our good. For our growth. For His glory.

ALSO LOOK AT 1 JOHN 3:16-18.

What have you seen happen in the following situations?
Speaking the truth without any love:

Loving someone but not speaking the truth:

When both truth and love come together, what's the likely result?

Real love—love that desires what's best for someone else—does the hard work of peacemaking. Love swallows its pride, speaks the truth, and takes action to humbly confront sin. It does so knowing that any temporary discomfort pales in comparison to the eternal joy, freedom, and satisfaction found in a right relationship with our Redeemer.

The right motivation behind confronting sin must always be growth, health, and unity in the family of God.

READ MATTHEW 18:12-14.

What does Jesus' parable teach you about God?

What does it teach you about the way He views someone who's wandered away?

What does it teach you about reconciliation?

Jesus provided explicit instruction for the way relational sins and offenses should be handled among His family—in the life of His church. Later we'll look more at what happens if the person doesn't respond to what you humbly bring into the light.

READ MATTHEW 18:15.

What does Jesus teach as the first step in confronting someone's sin?

What's the desired outcome?

READ GALATIANS 6:1-4.

What warning is provided as you prepare to confront someone about their sin against you?

Think about a person who's sinned against you in some way, and you know this isn't a case you should simply absorb or overlook.

Have you already taken the log out of your own eye so that you can clearly see the speck in the eye of your brother or sister?

What's your purpose for talking with this person? Is it to restore him or her, to restore a relationship, to glorify God? Inspect your motives.

Have you prayed about this issue? Have you prayed for this person? Have you sought the leading of the Lord in this matter?

Write your plan for meeting one-on-one and talking with this person about the issue.

BEFORE MOVING FORWARD WITH SPEAKING THE TRUTH IN LOVE, BE SURE TO PRAY, GIVING THIS PROCESS TO GOD TO LEAD YOU THROUGH IT. ASK HIM TO HELP YOU WEIGH YOUR MOTIVES AND CLEAR YOUR HEART OF ANY BITTERNESS OR ANGER YOU MAY HOLD INSIDE. PRAY FOR THE PERSON WHO'S SINNED AGAINST YOU. PRAY FOR THIS PERSON'S HEART AND RECEPTIVITY. PRAY FOR RESTORATION.

10.3

WHEN THEY DON'T LISTEN

"If he listens to you, you have gained your brother" (Matt. 18:15). You've restored a relationship. Heaven celebrates—and so do you. But what if it doesn't happen like that? What if they dismiss your concern or even get defensive and angry? What if it only seems to pour fuel on the fire, and things are worse than before?

Jesus wasn't naive, believing everything would be perfect if we'd just work up the courage to call someone out in love. He provided step-by-step instruction on how things could escalate in conflict resolution.

It may get messy before it clears up. But the goal is to recover a relationship in the Father's family. Because the goal isn't just to get it off your chest but to labor for the restored heart of the other person, you can't just quit and write them off—not until they've given you no other option.

READ MATTHEW 18:15-17.

> To be clear, leaving no room to skip this step, what is always the starting point and the desired outcome of confronting sin (see v. 15)?

> This concept of bringing the matter before two or three witnesses was a part of Jewish law and was widely used in both the Old and New Testaments (see Deut. 19:15; John 8:17; 2 Cor. 13:1; 1 Tim. 5:19; Heb. 10:28). What purposes would it serve to bring another person or two with you to talk with someone who's sinned against you?

> Who comes to mind as individuals you could ask to go with you if you need support? Remember, the intent isn't to gang up on someone but to lovingly win a brother or sister back into a relationship, so these people must be trusted friends with the person's best interest at heart.

What happens then, if you, along with two other godly men or women of integrity, go to the person who's sinned against you, and that person says, "I hear you. I even see it in the Bible. But I don't care"? Well, it doesn't stop there. Then you take it to the church.

If the matter at hand is in your small group, how would you handle this step? Would you take this issue to the whole group, outside the group to a church leader, or to another individual or group of people who represent the church?

What leader(s) in your church would you seek out if the previous steps brought no reconciliation?

If, after each of the previous steps, all you get back in return for the painful persistence of your love is denial, stubbornness, or even anger, then put enough trust in the wisdom of Scripture to follow it through to the end Jesus prescribed.

As painful as this whole process can be—and this final step certainly is painful—it's vital that you recognize it's not personal. It's not about you. It's a matter of everyone submitting to the authority of Christ.

Now listen. This is tough.

When men and women who've said, "I'm a Christian" get to the place where they say, "Forget what the elders say; forget what the Bible says; I'm doing what I want," they're bearing the fruit of unbelief.

If a person refuses to listen to any inner conviction of the Spirit and the Word of God; the loving concern of a friend, supported then by several close friends; and ultimately the leadership of the church, that person is acting as an unbeliever and therefore should be treated as such.

Why? In hope that they will repent and manifest the reality of their saving faith.

Since your purpose is restoration, how do you explain this last step in the process?

Look again at the two parables that bookend this passage on dealing with sin in the church (Matt. 18:10-14,21-35). How do those two parables relate to church discipline?

The ultimate goal of confronting someone who's sinned against you is to bring glory to God. In what ways does this process glorify God, even if the person refuses to listen or be reconciled?

The longer you put this off, the harder it's going to be. And the harder it gets, the less likely you'll be to do it. And if you're pretty sure you're never going to put yourself at risk of being the bad guy like that—even at the cost of a spoiled relationship, even at the potential cost of leaving someone to struggle all alone with their sin—then you're walking against the current of redemption. You're standing in the way of freedom, both yours and theirs. You're settling for what the gospel's done for you without really caring about what it can do for someone else.

Isn't redemption worth an uncomfortable conversation? Worth losing a little sleep over? Is any price too great, really?

What if it were you? If your relationship with Christ and His church was hanging in the balance, wouldn't you want someone to call you out as you ran headlong down a dead-end path? Silence is a death wish. It's saying you don't care that someone's unaware of the danger they're in. Can you see that speaking up and reaching out are the only loving things to do?

END YOUR STUDY IN PRAYER, ONCE AGAIN PUTTING THIS PROCESS IN GOD'S HANDS. ASK FOR HIS POWER AS YOU ENTER THE PROCESS OF RECONCILING WITH SOMEONE WHO'S SINNED AGAINST YOU.

PURSUING JOY: THE ABUNDANT LIFE

SHARE WHAT GOD IS DOING. #RECOVERINGREDEMPTION

BEGIN YOUR SESSION WITH THE ACTIVITY BELOW.

> What did you learn about confronting sin in session 10?

> Would anyone be willing to share, without divulging names or breaking confidentialities, either your plans to meet with someone who's sinned against you or how an actual meeting went?

This sanctification process is a continual journey. Today we'll look at how to sustain our faith over the long run, particularly how to keep up the ongoing ethic of our daily confession, repentance, and doing life together.

> How have you been doing in these progressive steps of sanctification? Do you tend to be fairly consistent or go in spurts?

TO PREPARE FOR THE VIDEO, READ ALOUD HEBREWS 12:1-2:

> *Since we are surrounded by so great a cloud of witnesses, let us also lay aside every weight, and sin which clings so closely, and let us run with endurance the race that is set before us, looking to Jesus, the founder and perfecter of our faith, who for the joy that was set before him endured the cross, despising the shame, and is seated at the right hand of the throne of God.*

WATCH

COMPLETE THE VIEWER GUIDE BELOW AS YOU WATCH SESSION 11.

Our entire lives will be filled with confession, repentance, and life _____.

You do what you do because you think in doing them, you're going to be satisfied, you're going to find _____, you're going to experience joy.

Knowing and being reconciled to God in Christ is where the most _____ is experienced.

Real, deep, meaningful life is found in being _____ to the Son of God.

If we will persevere in the ongoing ethic of confession, repentance, and life together, we must be very serious about pursuing _____.

STEPS TOWARD JOY IN CHRIST

1. Ever-increasing, eternal, legitimate joy cannot be found outside a serious pursuit of a _____ with Jesus Christ.

Few things destroy idols like the desert, but let's make sure we're not in the desert by our own _____.

2. Put to death what is _____ in you.

We are given one offensive weapon with which to fight and put to death these things: the sword of the Spirit, the _____ of God (see Eph. 6:17).

When we walk into sin, we're believing the _____ that sin offers.

Unlike the promises of our flesh, God is able to _____ and _____ the promises He makes to His children (see 2 Cor. 1:20).

Everything that is pleasurable was created by God and gifted to man for God's _____.

3. We are now defined by Christ's _____ _____, not by our ethnicity, not by our socioeconomic status.

4. Become an expert in how _____ God has been to you.

Learn to walk in _____.

Video sessions available for purchase
at *www.lifeway.com/recoveringredemption*

DISCUSS THE VIDEO SEGMENT, USING THE QUESTIONS BELOW.

What jumped out to you in this message?

Matt made the jostling comment that we're all hedonists. *Hedonism* is a philosophy that asserts pleasure or happiness is the sole or chief good in life. Matt said a pursuit of pleasure drives everything we do. What's your reaction to this statement? What forms does the pursuit of pleasure take in our society? How do you pursue happiness in your life?

Matt gave four ways we can continue to sustain our faith and seek ever-increasing joy.

☐ Seriously pursue an ongoing relationship with Jesus Christ as your ultimate source of joy.

☐ Put to death what's worldly and a source of false joy.

☐ Live in unity and harmony with one another as God's family.

☐ Become an expert in God's goodness. Be thankful.

With which of these do you most struggle? Why?

How can we as a small group help you grow in these areas?

Which do you memorize more often—Bible verses revealing wickedness in our hearts (Matt used Job 31:1 as an example) or Scriptures that reveal the promises of God?

Matt asked, "What if we just fully believed God keeps His promises in a way sin cannot?" How would you answer that question?

As you close your time together in prayer, include a time to thank God for His many blessings in your lives.

READ SESSION 11 AND COMPLETE THE PERSONAL STUDY BEFORE THE NEXT GROUP EXPERIENCE.

CONSIDER GOING DEEPER INTO THIS CONTENT BY READING CHAPTER 12 IN MATT CHANDLER AND MICHAEL SNETZER'S BOOK RECOVERING REDEMPTION *(B&H, 2014).*

PURSUING JOY: THE ABUNDANT LIFE

Joy. We all want joy.

Everything you do in life stems from a desire to experience joy, pleasure, satisfaction, or relief. We're driven by the conviction, based on appetites living naturally inside the human heart, that certain actions will lead to happiness. We seek this satisfaction in all kinds of places. People eat and drink to pursue it. They have sex to pursue it. They go to the movies to pursue it. They play fantasy football to pursue it. They get married and have children to pursue it. They work 60 hours a week to pursue it. They go to the gym to pursue it. They go to church to pursue it.

Give us joy. We'll do *anything* for it.

The surprising reality is that this desire is a God-given gift.

And ultimately what we're seeking is found in the gospel.

This driving hunger is what fuels us to continually seek Christ—to persevere in the ongoing ethics of sanctification.

II.

MOTIVATED BY JOY

Regardless of how you've come to think about happiness and pleasure, God wired that desire in you. It's not a result of the fall. It's true that some twisted pursuits are broken and sinful, but the desire for pleasure is God-given. You were designed to be ultimately satisfied and happily dependent on your Creator.

The Bible is clear: our greatest joy is in Jesus.

Life with Him is better than anything else. Knowing Him and being reconciled to the Father through Him is the one way we find the most pleasurable, long-lasting, and irreplaceable joy known to humanity.

If it's still difficult to wrap your head around an innate godly desire for pleasure, let's examine the way Jesus defined His own life and ministry.

READ JOHN 10:10 AND WRITE IT BELOW.

What does this verse reveal about our deep desire for more in life?

What did Jesus identify as the only two possible outcomes to our pursuit of satisfaction?

READ PSALM 4:6-7 AND PROVERBS 8:19.

What do these passages tell you about the joy and life God gives, compared to what the world offers?

READ ECCLESIASTES 2:1-11.

Summarize, in your own words, the experience of Solomon, a man considered to be one of the wealthiest and wisest figures in history.

READ PSALM 16:11.

Where did King David find lasting pleasure and real joy?

Nothing in this world will ultimately satisfy. No amount of grain and wine (ancient symbols for wealth) will ever make you happy. Now the kings of Israel, men like David and his son Solomon, knew a thing or two about wealth, power, luxury, and achievement but concluded that no lasting joy or satisfaction could be found outside God. Ironically, Solomon's father had clearly identified the vanity of chasing the things of this world, but sometimes people need to come to this conclusion for themselves before they truly embrace it.

As we were cautioned with the crooked path of surface religion, pursuing the pride of godly achievements isn't the same as pursuing the joy of God Himself.

READ PHILIPPIANS 3:4-8.

If you put Paul's religious background in modern-day-church terms, how would you describe him?

What would Paul say brought him ultimate joy and worth?

Take Paul's experience (you can use Solomon's and David's experiences as well) and write your own statement about where your joy isn't based and where it is based. Use the starter sentence to help you begin:

Though I could have reason for confidence in the flesh (list personal accomplishments, religious honors, and achievements) …

I consider them …

as compared to …

If all our churchgoing, choir singing, check writing, and brownie baking don't serve their first and highest purpose by putting us more in love with Jesus, then, well … all that stuff isn't worth anything.

Compared to the infinite joy of knowing Christ, everything else is rubbish. Dung.

If the greatest tragedy of Eden was the loss of intimate fellowship with the Maker of our souls, the greatest joy of life in His kingdom is recovering this intimacy we lost.

And why should we expect anything else to rival this pleasure? Why would any other suitor seem a worthy competitor?

YOUR PRAYER FOR TODAY IS SIMPLE. TELL GOD YOU DESIRE TO FOLLOW HIM AS YOUR SOURCE OF REAL JOY AND ASK HIM TO HELP YOU SEE THE MEANINGLESSNESS OF THINGS—EVEN GOOD THINGS IN THIS WORLD THAT HE'S GIVEN YOU—THAT DON'T BRING LASTING JOY OR ABUNDANT LIFE.

ACCEPT NO SUBSTITUTES

The Christian life inevitably has ups and downs, highs and lows, including dry seasons when progress and growth seem to be lacking. While in these spiritual deserts, you feel lonely, exhausted, and distant from God. He may even seem unaware of and inattentive to your needs. But you're not the first to experience this phenomenon; this isn't new territory.

Many of our heroes in the Bible went through their own deserts. But like them, God, as an act of love, will lead you through those dry seasons to bring you to your knees, onto your face, and back to the only thing that can quench your thirst and bring you joy—Himself.

READ JEREMIAH 29:10-14.

What did God promise during an intense dry season?

How have you experienced burnout or dry seasons?

Growing in spiritual maturity includes growing in dependence upon God. You learn to distinguish between a desert that God's leading you through—destroying idols and instilling a deep thirst for Living Water—from willfully wandering back down crooked paths into selfishness and isolation, away from His righteousness, truth, and joy.

READ ROMANS 1:21-25.

What's the "exchange" people have made (vv. 23,25)?

What's the consequence of looking to things to give us joy that they ultimately cannot?

Go back and read verses 19-20. What legitimate excuses can we make for looking for joy in all the wrong places?

Read Romans 5:1-5. How did Paul describe our sources of joy?

Because at our core we're hedonists, when we walk into sin, we believe the promise it offers. But we must understand that these false pursuits of joy will never deliver on their promises. At their roots they're lies that can't support their own arguments. Christ, on the other hand, is all-powerful and perfectly good. He's the Vine in which we need to reroot ourselves to experience abundant life and produce fruit that pleases God.

Think of one area in your life where you tend to seek satisfaction through something that has no power to give it. Some examples are laziness; lust and sexual immorality; anger, bitterness, malice, rage, and wrath; cheating and stealing; gossip and slander; greed and covetousness.

The lie of this sin is:

Christ truly gives more abundant life and joy in this way:

Decide now how you'll respond when pulled toward this lie. I'll choose Christ by …

Have you tried memorizing Scripture that tells you not to do something wrong? How effective is that by itself?

Identifying the lie of sin and counterattacking with a greater joy found in Christ is a healthy battle plan. Too often Christians struggle with uprooting sin and combating its lies because we're not wielding the Sword well. By now you may know it isn't sufficient to simply memorize verses telling you not to do something (for example, see Job 31:1). These are good but not enough. We're hedonists, remember? We have to stop only playing defense and start taking an offensive stand.

READ EPHESIANS 6:11-17.

> The Sword of the Spirit—that is, the Word of God—is the only offensive weapon God gives Christians to conquer and put to death sin in our lives. What are some specific ways you can use the Word of God as an offensive weapon against the Devil's schemes?

> For each Scripture identify a lie to overcome and the promise of greater joy and satisfaction. How will you attack sin at its root?
>
> Psalm 36:7-9
>
> Psalm 37:4
>
> Proverbs 16:3
>
> Matthew 5:8
>
> Philippians 4:7
>
> James 1:12

What verse or verses would you add to this list, especially one that you need as an offensive weapon against the Devil's schemes in your life? Some Bibles include a topical index or even a Bible-promises section. You can also find books and apps that list Bible promises by topic.

THANK GOD FOR THE INCREDIBLE PROMISES OF HIS WORD. THANK HIM FOR MAKING A RELATIONSHIP WITH HIM POSSIBLE THROUGH JESUS' SACRIFICE—THE RELATIONSHIP THAT'S THE ONLY SOURCE OF YOUR ULTIMATE JOY.

11.3

EXPERTS IN GOD'S GOODNESS

Another way we stumble off course is also related to focus and settling. We drift away from the joy of Christ because we're drawn toward other—lesser—things.

Our default posture as human beings—as hedonists—is to want more. But in our selfishness this often warps into an acute sensitivity to what we don't have rather than an awareness of what's at our disposal. Even as Christ-followers, we compare what God, in His goodness and grace, has given to others with what He's given to us. As with our futile efforts to tip scales with religious morality, we start keeping score again, but this time it's not about what we've done, it's about what we have. We actually give God a scorecard. We scrutinize the scorecards to see how good (or bad) our life is in comparison to the lives of people around us.

But really? We've already seen that we're in desperate need for God's continual generosity and daily grace. He's been abundantly good to us.

And let's be straight: this is a dark place to live. How twisted are we to dwell on the things we don't have instead of enjoying the things we do have? We're not even being good hedonists!

It's time to change the way we think. No more junior-varsity hedonism, craving more of what we don't have. It's time to drink deeply, immersing ourselves in the gloriously satisfying gifts of the Father.

Become an expert in God's goodness.

> Read the following Scripture passages and write down what they teach you about God and ways you should respond. By the way, these would also make good memory verses.
>
> Psalm 23
>
>
> Psalm 119:9-24

Luke 19:10

John 3:16-17

Romans 8:26

Ephesians 3:6

2 Peter 3:9

We've been given the Holy Spirit to awaken our dead hearts. That's a joy. We've been justified and delighted in as adopted children of a Heavenly Father. Joy. We are coheirs with Jesus Christ. Joy. We've been given His Holy Word, revealing the infinite riches of the mystery found in the gospel. Joy. We've been given unlimited personal access to the King of the universe through prayer. Joy. We've been set free from the bondage of slavery—from the pursuit of a better *self*, affirmation from *others*, fleeting pleasures in *the world*, and performance-based moral *religion*. Joy. Abundant joy.

READ MATTHEW 13:44.

In what ways is the kingdom of heaven like the treasure buried in a field?

Honestly, is there anything in your life you wouldn't be willing to give up for the sake of the kingdom?

If the kingdom of God is worth cashing in everything—pursuing it regardless of the costs—what changes does that make in the current focus and direction of your life?

How does it change your view of temptation, guilt and shame, anxiety and fear?

How does that affect your spending and giving?

How does it change the way you treat other people?

Learn to walk in thankfulness. Learn to walk in gratitude. Everything about your understanding of God and your relationship with others will begin to change when you marvel at how good God is rather than obsess over what you don't have.

You shouldn't be a stranger to God's mercy and blessing in your life. You should be an expert in it. Are you struggling? Then lay that before the feet of God, voice that to your community of faith, and be serious about recognizing every way God has blessed you.

Why would anyone designed to pursue joy since the creation of the world, as we are, not want to be the most unabashed, undaunted, uninhibited seeker of pleasure that he or she could possibly be? As C. S. Lewis wrote in *The Weight of Glory*, "We are half-hearted creatures, fooling about with drink and sex and ambition when infinite joy is offered us, like an ignorant child who wants to go on making mud pies in a slum because he cannot imagine what is meant by the offer of a holiday at sea. We are far too easily pleased."[1]

Oh, let this not be said of us. God wants more for you—more of Him. And He's more than enough.

Make a list of all you have to be grateful to God for.

LOOK THROUGH THE LIST OF THINGS YOU'RE GRATEFUL FOR. AS YOU GO THROUGH IT, THANK GOD, THE GIVER OF ALL GOOD AND PERFECT GIFTS, FOR EACH ONE.

1. C. S. Lewis, *The Weight of Glory: And Other Addresses* (New York: HarperCollins, 1949), 26.

SHARING HOPE: LIGHT OF THE WORLD

BEGIN YOUR SESSION WITH THE ACTIVITY BELOW.

Session 11 concluded with a challenge to become an expert in God's goodness. What were you thankful for?

How did this positive outlook help you stay focused and motivated in your daily walk—the ongoing ethic of sanctification?

What else did you learn about being motivated by joy? Not settling for temporary substitutes? Using Scripture as an offensive weapon?

How do you see joy and gratitude tying together everything we've studied?

Today we'll wrap up everything we've studied in *Recovering Redemption*.

All this is not ultimately for our good alone; the world around us is also broken and desperately needs the same hope we've found in Christ.

TO PREPARE FOR THE VIDEO, READ ALOUD ISAIAH 42:6-7:

> *I am the LORD; I have called you in righteousness;*
>   *I will take you by the hand and keep you;*
> *I will give you as a covenant for the people,*
>   *a light for the nations,*
>   *to open the eyes that are blind,*
> *to bring out the prisoners from the dungeon,*
>   *from the prison those who sit in darkness.*

COMPLETE THE VIEWER GUIDE BELOW AS YOU WATCH SESSION 12.

"This is the light," outside the light of the gospel, becomes the grid by which people will actively oppress and operate in _____.

We can't fix our own issues. Our hope is rooted in the _____ alone.

Blessed are the ones who understand that they own nothing, possess nothing, have nothing that was not _____ to them by God.

Blessed are those who are aware of how they have rebelled against God, who are _____ in their sin, and who in their poor-in-spirit bankruptcy have _____ _____ to the Father.

Conviction from God is a _____ from God.

We understand fully that all we have and all that has been given to us has been given to us by _____. Therefore, we will be marked by a _____ and gentleness that are present because of our understanding of where all things came from.

The more of Jesus you experience, the more of Him you _____.

One of the things that comes in our lowliness, in our humility, in our dependence on God is a growing empathy and _____ for others.

A peacemaker refuses to let anyone sow seeds of _____.

We are a people commanded by God to be marked by love, compassion, patience, mercy, and _____.

We are a people who have been put in a precarious spot: to be _____ the world _____ the world.

HOW WE LIVE OUT BEING THE LIGHT

1. Follow the _____ that led you into the career you're in.

2. Within the domain God has placed you, systematically push back systemic _____.

DISCUSS THE VIDEO SEGMENT, USING THE QUESTIONS BELOW.

What stood out to you most in Matt's teaching?

What challenged you?

Jesus described a countercultural kingdom reality in the Beatitudes (see Matt. 5:1-11). With which one(s) do you struggle most? Why do you think that is? How can we as a group help you in that area?

What does it mean to be the light of the world (see Matt. 5:14-16)?

What's the most recent opportunity you've had to be the light of the world?

What does it look like for you to let your light shine in your workplace or school, in your neighborhood, in your family, in a recreational activity, or somewhere else?

Write the names of people who need Jesus and whom you sense God has put into your life—whether at work or school, parents of your children's friends, neighbors, people at the gym, etc. Quickly share with your group the people's names and where you know them from.

Conclude in prayer, thanking God that our eyes have been opened to the light of the gospel. Ask for help to see needs and opportunities all around us, specifically praying for the names everyone identified. Pray for joyful confidence in making a new habit of sharing the hope of Christ.

READ SESSION12 AND COMPLETE THE PERSONAL STUDY BEFORE THE NEXT GROUP EXPERIENCE.

CONSIDER GOING DEEPER INTO THIS CONTENT BY READING THE EPILOGUE IN MATT CHANDLER AND MICHAEL SNETZER'S BOOK RECOVERING REDEMPTION (B&H, 2014).

SHARING HOPE: LIGHT OF THE WORLD

Everyone needs the healing and freedom you have in Christ. You're a beacon of hope, pointing others to true joy and abundant life.

We began with the gospel, recognizing our brokenness and our need for healing and rescue. Our desire for satisfaction that can't be found in a better version of *ourselves*, the affirmation of *others*, pleasures of *the world*, or active moral *religion* is found only in Christ. Through faith in Him, evidenced by repentance, we're immediately justified and adopted by God.

We then entered an ongoing process of sanctification, throwing off all hindrances and reconciling our vertical relationship with God and horizontal relationships with others. Our new life is motivated by joy, as we endure the highs and lows of the daily grind. All this isn't ultimately for our good alone; the world around us is also broken and desperately needs the same hope we've found in Christ.

It's not prideful to recognize that everyone needs what we have.

It's the humble truth, because we did nothing to earn the favor of God. By grace we are saved. Christ gave His life willfully, freely, and generously. We now share the life we have in Him the same way.

WHO IS THE LIGHT?

"Let there be light" (Gen. 1:3). God started creating with these four words. And it was good. This is how everything started. But it didn't stay that way. In Genesis 3 people first chose darkness instead of light. Doubting God's goodness, they fell for a lie and sought satisfaction outside a relationship with their Creator—with the things He created. They went into hiding as a new disorder came shuddering into their lives—guilt and shame, fear and anxiety, blame and pain, avoidance and aggression, sin and ultimately death.

But God had a plan. He would recover what was lost. Just as the first creation started with light, the new creation began with a Light that would shine in the darkness. And this would change everything.

> Record what each passage adds to your understanding of Jesus' role as Light in a dark world. Also note ways people responded to this Light.
>
> John 1:1-14
>
>
>
> John 3:19-21
>
>
>
> John 8:12
>
>
>
> John 9:5
>
>
>
> John 12:44-47
>
>
>
> 1 John 1:5-7

READ 2 CORINTHIANS 4:1-6.

What's the tactic of the Enemy—the god of this world—Satan?

What's our mission, despite the Enemy's strategy?

Having experienced Christ, we joyfully worship Him in plain view of a world that needs His light. Empowered by the Holy Spirit, we bring a comprehensive gospel to that world—a message demonstrated by our deeds and proclaimed through our words—with the goal of glorifying God by making disciples of Jesus Christ.

In this way we manifest Christ in our world. As the Father sent Him as the Light into the world, so He sends us into the world to be light in the darkness (see John 17:12-21).

READ MATTHEW 5:14-16.

What does it look like to let your light shine before others?

How have you hidden your light rather than letting it shine?

Because Jesus is the source of the light we're to shine—in other words, we don't shine our own light but reflect His—what encouragement does that give you in being a light in the darkness?

What excuses does it eliminate?

Only a gross misunderstanding of the gospel would make us want to keep His glory hidden within us, to have this flame of His presence blazing inside and yet to fearfully "put it under a basket" (v. 15).

READ EPHESIANS 5:8-21.

> What does this passage teach you about how to be a light in a world of darkness?

READ PHILIPPIANS 2:12-16.

> What attitudes are vital for being a light in the darkness?

> What lessons from the previous 11 sessions come to your mind as you apply these verses about shining brightly?

Jesus is the Light. Because He's in us, we are the light. Our hope is in the gospel alone. When Jesus said, "You are the light of the world" (Matt. 5:14), He wasn't talking about people who've bought into civil religion or cultural Christianity but those who've legitimately been transformed by the gospel and are His disciples. The redeemed.

TAKE A MOMENT TO PRAISE GOD AS THE CREATOR OF THE UNIVERSE, THE CREATOR OF LIGHT AND ALL THAT'S GOOD. PRAISE HIM FOR JESUS, WHO CAME AS THE LIGHT INTO A WORLD FULL OF DARKNESS. CONFESS THE TIMES YOU'VE RECENTLY DECIDED TO WALK IN DARKNESS RATHER THAN LIGHT. BRING YOUR SIN INTO THE LIGHT; LET IT BE EXPOSED BY THE LIGHT. PROFESS YOUR DESIRE TO LIVE AS A CHILD OF LIGHT AND YOUR NEED FOR HIS SPIRIT TO ACCOMPLISH THAT. ASK HIM FOR OPPORTUNITIES TODAY TO BE HIS LIGHT IN THIS DARK WORLD.

COUNTERCULTURAL WISDOM

If Jesus is the answer to all the world's problems, but the world is looking in all the wrong places for a solution, then those of us who follow Him will stand in stark contrast to the wisdom of the world, even other world religions. We may look crazy (see Acts 26:24; 2 Cor. 5:13). But the world is heading down dark, dead-end paths. The Light has revealed a new direction—the Way—a trajectory toward abundant life. Look at what God does in the hearts of those who believe—how He transforms our character using a logic that turns the wisdom of this world on its head.

READ MATTHEW 5:1-6.

The religious leaders of Jesus' day taught that righteousness could be measured by externals, like how you prayed, how much you gave, or how often you fasted. How did Jesus describe righteousness?

To the disciples who heard Jesus' message, the word *blessed* meant more than just *happy*. It meant the divine joy or inner satisfaction a believer could have, regardless of circumstances. What have you learned so far that helps you understand this concept of being blessed?

Let's unpack these Beatitudes. As you read each description and supporting Scripture, consider how these first four encourage a dependence on the Lord. For each one, write an observation or application. What does this look like in your life?

POOR IN SPIRIT. Blessed are those who understand that they're spiritually bankrupt, that they need help. If you're so awesome that you don't need a Savior, then you're not saved. (See Rom. 12:3.)

Observation/Application:

THOSE WHO MOURN. Blessed are those who are aware of how they've rebelled against God, who are heartbroken in their sin, and who in their bankruptcy have cried out to the Father. Don't despise conviction. It's a gift from God. (See Luke 18:13.)

Observation/Application:

THE MEEK. Blessed are those who humbly acknowledge that all we have has been given to us by God. A sincere gentleness is present when we recognize that nothing in our own strength has ever helped anything. This isn't passivity; this is confidence in the surpassing greatness of God. (See Phil. 4:5.)

Observation/Application:

THOSE WHO HUNGER AND THIRST. Blessed are those who still want more of the Lord—who want to experience more of His grace, to walk in more of His power, to understand Him more fully, to obey Him more passionately, to follow Him with greater resolve. The more of Jesus you experience, the more of Him you want. Though completely satisfied, you desire more of the inexhaustible fountain of grace. (See Ps. 42:1-2.)

Observation/Application:

Are you experiencing these blessings? In which of these do you need to grow?

The next three Beatitudes move from our dependence on God to its outworking in our daily lives—the horizontal overflow of a right vertical relationship.

READ MATTHEW 5:7-9.

What characteristics stand out most to you? How are these countercultural?

THE MERCIFUL. Blessed are those who have a growing empathy and compassion for others. Our posture is never one of judgment; our posture is always one of empathy, compassion, patience, love. That's the default posture of the sons and daughters of God because we've been forgiven of much. (See Ps. 112:4.)

Observation/Application:

THE PURE IN HEART. Blessed are those with nothing to hide—exposed but unashamed. They take every thought captive under Christ, lay it at the feet of the Father, confess that they don't want that thought to be in their lives, ask for pure thoughts and pure motives, ask for His forgiveness, rest in the forgiveness they know He lavishes on them, and move forward. (See 1 Pet. 1:22.)

Observation/Application:

THE PEACEMAKERS. Blessed are those who refuse to let anyone sow any seeds of disunity. They not only keep peace by resolving conflicts that arise, but also proactively engage others for the sake of building up unified community. A peacemaker risks conflict for the sake of peace. (See Jas. 3:18.)

Observation/Application:

In which of these do you need to grow?

Jesus took a turn here in the Beatitudes, and what He said next was counterintuitive—as if everything up to that point hadn't already flown in the face of cultural norms. But this is real-world encouragement from Jesus.

READ MATTHEW 5:10-12.

What does it mean to be persecuted "for righteousness' sake" (v. 10) rather than for another reason?

What kinds of accusations do you see and hear in today's culture against Christians and Christianity?

We're a people commanded by God to be marked by love, compassion, patience, mercy, and hospitality. Even when persecuted, slandered, and reviled, we don't build walls; we open doors. What effect can our loving attitudes and actions have on people, even in the midst of persecution?

Embodying the attitudes of Christ—living by this ongoing kingdom ethic—will set you in stark contrast to the world around you. It will turn heads; people will even look at you sideways. If you're not dialed in to the growing hostility and marginalization of Christianity from mainstream culture, you're just not paying attention.

It's increasingly unpopular to hold confidently to the truth of the gospel. Your neighbors, coworkers, and family members should be so confused by the jarring inconsistency between any preconceived ideas about narrow-minded, judgmental, Christian intolerance and the faith, hope, and love of Jesus shining from your life that they have to ask what's really going on. You are the light of the world—a city on a hill. Let the freedom and hope of redemption surprise the world around you.

PRAISE GOD FOR HIS BLESSINGS, EVEN THOSE THAT SEEM, BY WORLDLY STANDARDS, TO BE CURSES. ASK GOD FOR MORE OF HIM AND FOR GROWTH IN THESE KINGDOM ATTRIBUTES.

PUSHING BACK DARKNESS

Before God laid the foundations of the earth, He chose us, the church, to live as instruments of grace in a lost, sin-darkened world (see Eph. 1:1-14). Our task is to be the light—to bear witness to God's wisdom and power through the gospel of Jesus.

We're called to give everything we have to this mission so that individuals God has put into our lives and in our communities and in the world will encounter the good news and be forever changed. Like candles positioned throughout a dark room, we've been strategically placed—by God's sovereign design—as light pushing back darkness.

This call may or may not lead us to foreign cultures across the ocean, but it will always call us to be intentional and available whenever, wherever, and with whomever God opens a door.

But, we build walls around ourselves, keeping a safe distance from what we consider to be the dangerous fringes of the general—sinful—population. It's time to believe enough in the power of the gospel that we will launch ourselves through any door God opens. Be confident that He can accomplish great things—not just because we're there but because He's with us.

> Think about where God has placed you: in your family; in your job, school, or neighborhood; or even in your small group. How have you been a light in the darkness within that domain?

> Whom have you closed yourself off from—judging them as too dark or too far gone? Whom should you prayerfully consider opening up to with godly wisdom?

In the small-group session you were asked to record the names of people who don't yet know Christ. List these names and any others that come to mind, below.

In what specific ways will you love, serve, encourage, or care for each of these people this week?

Trust the Spirit to lead you to the right people, at the right place, at the right time. When you open yourself up to the will of God, your life takes on true meaning and purpose. Christ changes everything.

READ MATTHEW 10:7-8.

What did Jesus' instructions to His disciples reveal about freely giving what has been received by explicitly sharing the gospel in both word and deed?

READ LUKE 4:16-21.

How did Isaiah's prophecy, which Jesus read, define Jesus' life and ministry?

How does it, therefore, define your life and ministry?

READ MATTHEW 25:35-40.

What did Jesus say about horizontal relationships reflecting our vertical relationship?

What kinds of people does Jesus call us to love and serve?

What ministries can you get involved in to help hurting people in your church, neighborhood, or city?

READ 1 JOHN 4:7-21.

How can our relationships with others make the gospel visible?

Whatever activities and interests fill up the 120 hours or so each week when you're not sleeping, they should all be saturated in the gospel. You've been placed in neighborhoods, workplaces, and communities as a light. But it's bigger than just the one-on-one interactions you have for the sake of the gospel. In each domain where God has placed you, you join the people of God—His church—in systematically pushing back darkness. This is all part of God's plan of redemption.

So whether you're in the realm of education, finance, government, agriculture, art, homemaking, or anything else, God has uniquely wired you and positioned you to share the gospel with individuals and to push back what is dark in the world. So, "let your light shine before others, so that they may see your good works and give glory to your Father who is in heaven" (Matt 5:16).

You were designed for this purpose. If you still need help identifying specific ways you can be intentional in sharing the hope of the gospel, consider the following questions.

READ COLOSSIANS 3:17.

What are you good at or passionate about?

Where do you spend your time? Think through your weekly schedule, identifying each physical location, maybe specific names of people you interact with, and the amount of time invested there each week.

How will you intentionally use those locations and activities—even those that aren't overtly spiritual—as platforms to shine the light of Christ like a city on a hill?

PRAY FOR THE INDIVIDUALS YOU LISTED WHO DON'T YET HAVE A SAVING RELATIONSHIP WITH CHRIST. PRAY THAT GOD WILL GIVE YOU OPPORTUNITIES TO LOVE AND SERVE THEM AND TO BE A LIGHT FOR THEM. ALSO PRAY FOR OTHER OPPORTUNITIES TO LOVE PEOPLE AND SERVE THROUGH YOUR CHURCH AND IN YOUR COMMUNITY, SHOWING THE LOVE OF GOD TO A DARK WORLD THAT DESPERATELY NEEDS HIS LIGHT AND SALVATION.

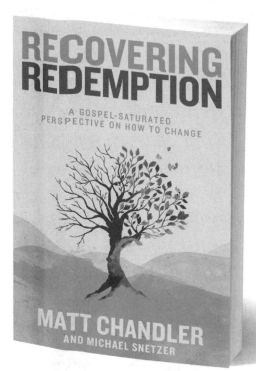